JOSHUA THE SPY

BOOK ONE

J.M. NAVON

JOSHUA THE SPY

BOOK ONE

J.M. NAVON

Medcibo Co. Publishers

DEDICATION

To my sister Dora who I see an image of Sarah, Abraham's wife, a strong and spiritual woman who kept many Bibles at her bedside and succumbed to pneumonia seven times until she finally passed away.

To my father David, who struggled with Multiple Sclerosis and never accepted Jesus as his Lord and Savior, and died not knowing him.

To my Mother Ida, who when I see her eyes, I see an image of Mary, the mother of Jesus, who cared for and loved her beloved son.

And finally, I dedicate this book t my daughter Leila, who supported and encouraged me through the writing process.

"Humanity is on a course of ultimate corruption and destruction."
.....Good must always conquer Evil.....

J.M. Navon

INTRODUCTION

It was a time God had finally decided upon leaving humans be, and casting a blind eye upon their transgressions. His son, Jesus Christ's crucifixion on the cross of Calvary to shed his blood and cleanse humanity of their sins had come to nothing but an act not appreciated by men, and it saddened God beyond expressions.

He had finally decided upon letting them defend and cater for themselves, without his intervention and guidance as he had so always done, since they couldn't tear themselves away from the lust their flesh brought them, and the sins humanity drowned in without a care in the world for what was wrong or what was right.

It was an era where injustice, murder, adultery, fornication, deceit and every other fruit of the devil and its seeds aired more than oxygen itself between the humans, rendering them impossible to pity, or even worthy of his love and compassion. Men and women did as they pleased, and taught their children in ways that differed from his preaching and words.

It was a difficult task to decide upon, but He finally chose to and turned his back on them.

For the first time, God finally decided to leave the world in the hands of the humans threatening to bring about their doom. His ears will remain deaf to them, and his eyes will cast no sight upon their actions, for they sore them and brought him nothing but ache towards his creations.

His decision to let humans into thousands of years of seclusions from him, left them to rampage towards doom and disobedience. However, he permitted his angels into the world of men, on occasions to perform miracles and to enable the heart of men to know still there is a presence more significant than any other up above; that He is still reigning and there was and will always be God.

Amongst the select group of angels chosen to mediate between his presence and existence with the humans was Satan whom God bestowed with the sole responsibility, dominion and power to rule over the corrupt world, like Satan had become, as a means of punishing those who still chose to ignore His words and existence.

Satan's job was to bring with him, enough affliction, pain, atrocities and every wormy experience he could bestow upon the sinners who defied God's words and desires. His task was one he was mandated to take seriously and not hold back, provided the stubborn heart of men remained stone hard and without repentance.

God kept tabs on things going on, while he kept his distance from men though, through constant feedback from his angels to ascertain whether or not the heart of men had turned around to him, but on numerous occasions, the reports of their defiance and sinful nature only seemed worse than it had been before. They weren't repentant, and couldn't stop themselves from drowning in immoral acts.

God himself, through these reports, had begun conceding the thoughts of laying waste to the entire world and destroying every creation in it as he did in Sodom and Gomorrah after their wrong ways had prompted him to bring an end to their existence with a lift of just His finger.

It was a decision he knew would bring him nothing but heartache should he go ahead to do it, but would be justified should it eventually come to be. A plan was in place — his decision final. His angels brought back some good news.

"Dear God, we believe there are some humans down there who still hold you in great regard, pray, worship and cherish you," Angel Gabriel reported with a bow before his throne after a journey to earth one day. "I believe there could be hope for them my Lord."

God gave it some serious thought, wondering how accurate those men's hearts could be. God decided he needed to see for himself through his son's eyes. He wanted to know what the heart of men held and what they were doing.

"Call me my son," he ordered, sending for the one person he could trust with the job.

He waited not long enough before the young frame walked into the large hall where his Father sat upon his mighty throne. His long brown hair shone in the presence of his holy light, while his manicured beard provided his face enough handsomeness impossible to match by any other. He walked towards his Father with his hand strengthened by the long, wooden acacia walking cane in his left hand, and his loyal angel, Michael on his right as they shortened the distance between himself and God in the mighty room.

He donned his brown shroud and hooded head cover, with the amulet given to him upon his birth, of him as a child sitting on his mother's legs, perfectly ringed around his neck. The amulet, made of bronze and approximately two inches and 5 cm in size, shaped in an octagon had on one side, a relief of when he was a child, and bearing, on the other hand, another of Angel Michael wielding his sword and slaying Satan himself.

The gift, which was from the three kings who had visited him upon his birth, and were now surrounding him, they had presented to commemorate his birth and offer protection, shone in beauty as he journeyed forward to his father.

"I hear you've called upon me my father?" God's son asked with a bow

"Yes, I have something important I need of you my dear son," God responded, standing up from his throne to meet eye to eye with his son. "I need you to go down to earth, and confirm if the heart of men is still true and just to my name," he asked of his son with his hands on his shoulders.

"But father, I'm not to appear until the end time as the book of Revelations stated," he reminded his father with a curious look across his face.

God smiled from the corner of his lips before responding.

"I know son, which is why they must never know who you truly are, and you will take another name. Like the 12 spies Moses used, you will be mine and report your findings to me," God explained to his son.

He knew he couldn't disobey his father, and he alone could get the job done without compromise. He had been amidst men and had seen firsthand what they were, but now he had to go back once again, but not as whom he was. He thought of the best outfit to suit his age and look, being 34 years of age.

"I shall take my leave immediately," God's son spoke in assurance, turning around to prepare for the mission his father had bestowed upon him.

He set out shortly after, with a perfect disguise, in blue jeans, a white shirt laced with blue and white fringes called a tzitzit. He knew the humans expected his coming as stated by the book of Revelations about the end time, but none of them knew when.

To the modern world, he was known as Jesus, and some who prefer to call him by his biblical name, Yeshua (ישוע), Yahshua, Yahushua, Yehovah, among other titles. Upon his death, where he was crucified, above him, a wooden plaque was nailed to the wood just a few inches above his head, which was also his burial headstone, and had read INRI short for the Latin phrase of Jesus Nazarenus Rex Iudaeorum,' meaning 'Jesus of Nazareth, King of the Jews.

CHAPTERS

CHAPTER 1

⁂

rrival of the Spy...
On a quiet night, the skies above were filled with
stars illuminating brightly and beautifully, amidst the
silence upon the fields on which no animals were grazing or feeding,
the calm and serenity of things were visible as one distinct star stood
out amongst the others in the sky. The moon shone in beauty as well,
bearing its alluring blue rim just in perfect sync with the stars' glow
up above.

The constellation above made a beautiful view for those who
dwelled their lives upon watching the stars and making meaning of
it. It held within its display an even more beautiful alignment than
any to be seen in months before. It was a clear night unlike any
other, and the fresh air made it feel even more special unlike any
other that had passed days before. Everything looked framed within
the definition of normal, and all was as it had always been, until a
strange occurrence began high up above, beyond the clouds, and
embedded almost in the heavens.

It all began with the most dazzling of the stars high up above, which stood in uniqueness, and had shone brightly amongst its peers. It had started spinning wildly in an odd manner, which it continued to do for the next few minutes before the transformation in a bright flash of shooting star falling at a rapid rate unlike any normal star does when it falls.

Breaking the silence was the melodic, ear-pleasing and alluring choir of angels singing loudly "Om So Hum Mantra." The pace of the shooting star heightened with the tempo of the song being sung aloud in heavenly melody took to its peak, as he descended upon the earth at an alarming rate. Those who were, fortunately, groping their telescopes might have been lucky enough to witness the shooting star, but most were asleep, unaware of the phenomenon occurring through the dead of the night, deep until morning began to rear its head.

The shooting star finally made its descent upon the earth, crashing hard upon the vast and silent field, with nobody in sight to see it happen. An air of smoke rose from the spot, with fumes emanating into the air like a spaceship had just crash landed and the gas fumes from its explosions had gotten into the air.

Joshua arriving

The rise of the morning sun coincided with the crawling of a man out the crash site, where the shooting star had made contact with the earth. He held in his hand a cane made of acacia wood, and looked nothing like a man who had just descended from dangerous heights into the soil. He seemed unharmed, untainted and as clean as one who had just exited the morning shower.

The sunrise which had begun appearing at the foot of the mountain, finally shed more illumination on the strange man all donned in weathered blue jeans, a plain white shirt and a brown cotton hoodie above his head, He had on his neck, a bronze amulet with an embedded image which looked worn and equally faded, but still providing a good view of the pictures on it, one of which was that of his mother, Mary Magdalene and three kings, as well as another of the angel Michael slaying Satan with his long and mighty sword.

Finally getting up on his feet, while slightly hunched against his acacia cane, his average height provided him just enough view of the site of his crash, where he had crawled out from to gain a better perspective of the mountain, as well as the environment, which his landing had restructured powerfully.

With a slight smile across his lips, he cast his gaze upon the horizon up ahead, where the rising sun had begun illuminating perfectly, to provide him with an unparalleled view of the beautiful lands and mountains over the horizon and before him. The mountains in his view ranged in height, mirroring the one on which cliff he stood, as well as others differing in height and size along the extended terrain.

He satisfied his eyes, and began the descent down into the valley, in a slow, but a necessary move that brought with it a feeling of rush within his young body, and reminded him of the fact that he was just a few years into his thirties. His limp hindered the natural spring in his steps, but he managed just fine and enough to get down to the valley where he heard the melodic tune of birds chirping.

The shadowy figures flew up above him, chirping and singing away, while he cast his gaze upon them with one hand flattened out above his eyes to keep out the intrusive sunlight. The birds flew past him without bother, just before a strange noise came from nearby and a bush had begun moving but with no sight of what made the branches swerve.

He walked closer to satisfy his curiosity, just within the same period a large white-tailed deer buck with pointed antlers jumped out of the bush and startled him to a scramble backward with his cane in hand. He could feel his heart pounding as he chuckled and tried desperately to calm himself.

The deer remained still, as it gazed upon the man in a powerful gaze and stance while wearing a majestic rack and aura around it as well. He seemed to be fascinated by the strange man, who had calmed himself and raised his hand towards the majestic deer.

"Go in peace now," he said in his first few words, that came easing past his lips, just as the deer obeyed and galloped away out towards the pasture.

CHAPTER 2

J oshua *meets Sarah*

He continued his walk through the shrubs, gently following a path, he could tell been previously created by people who legged it through. His journey would take no less than a few more minutes, underneath the brimming and beaming sun, which was now in full stare down upon the earth.

In the distance, just ahead of the shrubs he had come through unscathed, was a church, small in size, but evident to his function, with the sign of a cross extended just upon the roof to be seen well enough from a distance. The building itself was structured from wooden logs, and its cross was fashioned from the same timber that made up the four walls of the church. It remained unpainted but held itself in beauty from the lovely planks it had been constructed.

He smiled as he walked towards the structure. Surrounding the church, was a wooden fence, overlooking the Teton Mountain Range. The shortened distance between himself and the church, brought to his ears, the voices of the choir singing aloud, while men, women, and children jollied in song along with them. He hurried his steps further through the dirt-laden walkway and then a wooden walkway, bringing him closer to the entrance into the church where a wooden sign with words on it stood.

It read; "The Chapel of the Transfiguration, built in 1925," in plain white letterings upon a red wooden background to properly illuminate its wordings. He walked past the sign, and came across a huge door, wooden in nature, and slammed shut while those within went about their business.

Gently, he helped himself with the door, pulling it open with one hand, while the other supported his cane and his body to stand. He walked in slowly to the absent attention of the worshippers who initially hadn't realized his presence, and were still engrossed in their business of worship.

Silently, with the tapping of his acacia wooden walk stick against the wooden floorboard, whose sound got consumed by the loud chorus from their songs and voices, he journeyed his way through the tightly packed church, walking down the aisle as the worshippers began providing him with their attention. One after the other, their gazes stuck on him like glue as he made his lonely walk toward the altar.

Whispers began to air, in inquisition about the strange man. In a church as small as theirs, it was evident everyone knew everybody, and a peculiar face would stick out like a sore thumb.

"Who is he?" he could hear a lady whisper to her colleague, as the heightened sound of their worship song had lowered drastically due to his presence.

"I don't think he is from around here from the looks of it," another said; this time is coming from a teenager who shot him a bewildered gaze, before asking another question. "Why is he wearing a white shirt with fringes around his waist?"

He paid them no attention, choosing to focus on the intent within his heart in the house of God. He had walked in without a care for his differing, or the fact that the congregation saw him as different. He didn't see or portray himself as unusual because he was new in the church's vicinity and amongst its members, but of the same mind because he too had come to worship God, and in that, he was most welcomed and always would be.

He had heard some whisper about him not having a bible, but their ignorance brought nothing but a whisker of a smile to him; for he knew every word within the Holy Book and had them ingrained in him as life itself, thereby having no such need to go about with one. The words within the bible were more familiar to him than they could ever understand.

Making his walk well into the church, to his left, just in the middle of the church itself, was an empty seat, beside a similarly curious looking woman, who watched him occupy it and bow his head to pray afterward. She lingered her gaze on him for a short while, before turning it to the Pastor, who had begun his sermon. He too ended his prayer briefly and started to listen intently and with intensity.

The Pastor was giving his sermon about "The Gospel of Luke." It was one he knew, and had an interest in, while the large framed man spoke with eloquence, and captivated his congregation's attention and some made quick notes of his words.

The sermon brought a sudden warm feeling within him, seeping in slowly with images of his brothers; James, Joseph, Simon, and Judas. He relived the moment they were playing hide and seek with his head throbbing like he was drowning in a liquid of memory, but without the pains of being immersed and submerged in water coming with them.

"Where are you Jeshua?" they said, while he hid behind a large boulder?

The memory was clear as day, and he could tell he had chosen the spot so they wouldn't see him. He had cloaked himself with a camouflage, which made them doubt his presence even while standing just before him. In a sudden burst to life, revealing himself from his covering, they came running towards him with a hug.

"How come we couldn't see you hiding there?" Simon asked explicitly, wearing a curious look across his face.

"Yes, we searched all around but didn't find you," Joseph repeated his brother's words.

He chuckled loudly at their failed attempts and stood up before explaining to them;

"My cloak is like that of a chameleon's, and it blends with the boulder," he explained to their interesting faces.

He had just taken a few steps when the images in his head got flushed away, and his consciousness returned to his current surroundings, in which a rock band was playing a song on the stage. He rubbed his eyes to gain proper composure of himself, as the band played the song titled "I Surrender," while the entire church sang along joyfully. Joshua fixed his eyes on the men strumming their guitars singing about him, which brought joy to his ears. He said to himself, "Wow, they made a song about me, how creative" "that is a beautiful song," and he began to smile and nod his head showing approval.

The song began lifting peoples spirits, prompting them to stand up and wave their hands in the air calling out to him, and chanting the words "I surrender...I surrender". After they finished their song, they began to sing another one, "Here I am to worship." "Who is here to worship," the lead singer said. Everyone in the congregation said out loud, "We are." As he sang the song halfway, a woman joined him in a duet. Her voice was rich and powerful, and it beamed across the chapel, leaving the congregation mesmerized in a spiritual high.

Joshua could make out a set of seven band players, while the lead singer walked forward to introduce himself. He was a lanky, tall framed, handsome guy, with dark, short looking hair and brown eyes. His unique voice resonance across the room, and as he spoke, he had a commanding presence. It was apparent he was one for the crowd as cheers met his speech.

"Hello everyone, my name is Bret, and I play the six-stringed guitar, as the lead singer of the band," he said, introducing himself, before doing the same about his colleagues.

"Behind me is my bass player James," "on the electric guitar is Paul," "on the drum is Bill, on the steel guitar Chris, keyboardist John, and my expert fiddler, Michael."

To his side, was a blonde looking woman with medium long hair wearing a cotton Pancho with tassels and over the knee boots with tights. He introduced the lady by the name Jill as his backup singer and a solo singer as well. Bret went on ahead to continue singing, before coming to an end briefly, to the raucous applause of everyone who had listened, as well as the Pastor. It was evident they had sung well, which they accepted with beaming faces, just as the congregation sat down back into their chairs.

The Pastor continued from where he had left off on his sermon.

"We had the privilege of baptizing a few members of the church last week," he said.

He immediately motioned for the team to his left to display the footage of the baptized members on a projector and a large sheet cast on the wall behind him, bringing the images into full view for those within the church to see and have a glimpse of the occurrence as it had unfolded.

"Their names are Brad Lee, Ed Martin, Carla Martinez, Samantha Stone, and Sarah Abrams," he announced proudly to the cheers of the church members.

He looked over to Sarah, who was the lady seated by him who had turned to have a quick look at him as well before he smiled and gave her a nod of approval for her baptism. She smiled in return, gushing red where she sat, before turning her face away from his, as he did the same. They listened to the Pastor, who had continued as the video behind him came to a close.

"We always welcome those who are ready and willing to get baptized and become members of our church," the Pastor smiled along, before waving his hands to ask them all up on their feet. "Can we now rise to say the last prayer please," he sought of them? The entire church did as they were told.

"Now, I want each of you to look at the person sitting next to you, and those surrounding you, introduce yourself to them and shake their hands, ask how they are doing, and meet them like you would a loved one," he demanded further.

He had just turned to Sarah, who sat by him when she extended her hand to meet with his. She felt a warm and possessed feeling. Joshua noticed a unique smile with an equal set of dimples denting her cheeks in beauty. Her hair was a light blonde and her eyes blue like lapis lazuli. Her face was white and rosy. She wore a blue pastel dress.

"Hello, my name is Joshua Elo," he said, introducing himself as she acknowledged with a nod and a smile.

"I'm Sarah Abrams," she replied immediately.

"Yes, I know your name already, from the baptism images earlier," Joshua informed her.

Her face flushed red again immediately, blushing aloud for him to see as blood rushed into her cheeks. She turned away slightly before speaking;

"It's nice to meet you, Joshua," she struggled to voice. "You're welcome, Sarah," he responded, turning around to greet some more people, whom he told his name was Joshua Elo. The other church members were more than receptive to him, and he liked that pretty much. Immediately after the greetings, they tendered grace and prayers. He had just moved out of his seat to take his leave when Sarah called unto him;

"Joshua Elo," she pronounced his name in full, watching the man slowly turn around. "I'm certain I've never seen you around here before, if I may ask, what brings you to these parts?"

Joshua gently nodded in acknowledgment, staring her right back in the face, while she shifted her head to the side in shyness once more before he began speaking. He could read the body signs and could very much tell she was the shy kind.

"You're right Sarah," he began with, watching her gain some better composure. "I'm not from this world, but I came to seek work," he explained.

Her next actions made him ponder. She burst into laughter, looking more comical than what he had said. He did not realize why he tickled her ribs but guessed it had something to do with what he said.

Getting herself better composed and laughing less, she asked; "What world would that be, Mars?"

It finally dawned on Joshua that he had been the substance for his jest. He coughed slightly, clearing his throat.

"I'm sorry, you mistook my words," he apologized. "What I meant to say, is that I am not from this area."

Sarah listened more seriously this time around but looked a tad down upon hearing his wish.

"I'm sorry you might be disappointed, Joshua," she voiced in a down tone.

"Why is that?" he inquired?

"We don't have jobs around here, but perhaps the Pastor could help you get one, while I'd also ask around," she informed him.

A man walked over to them, interrupting their conversation, without intending to be rude.

"Joshua, this is John, he is the Head of the New Membership Committee," said Sarah.

"First-time visitors to our congregation are most welcomed and appreciated," he said, exchanging a brief handshake with Joshua. "So that we may know who you are and how we can assist you, would you please fill out the welcome card and place it on the plate while my assistants are passing it around?" he asked kindly, tending the form into Joshua's hand.

Joshua took a brief look at it before hearing the man speak once more.

"If you make a prayer requests, please write them down as well," he continued. "We appreciate your offering because it will help us tremendously paying for our church expenses," he finally ended his words.

He provided Joshua a pencil to go with the form in his hands, before excusing himself, indicating that he had an important meeting. The Pastor informed the church that next weeks sermon, they will cover the book of Hebrews, before dismissing the church's congregation.

~

Sarah turned to Joshua. "It is almost lunchtime, and I am getting a little bit hungry, would you care to join me for lunch at the town café?" she asked persuasively. "Jackson Hole, Wyoming has a nice little café called Café Genevieve, and it's a nice place," she tried harder to sell the idea of dining with him.

"I will be very much pleased," Joshua replied. Looking at the welcome card, he said. "I have to fill this out first," he informed her, taking his time to do it. Joshua took the yellow pencil that was given to him and licked the graphite tip with his mouth. He began to write his name on it. When he saw the word 'address,' he began to scratch his head with the pencil and said to himself, "Hmm unknown for now." Phone number and email. "unknown as well," he said. Your affiliation to a church? Joshua slowly mumbled and wrote on the card "Synagogue of Capernaum." Sarah patiently waited for him to fill out the card and smiled at him while he completed the last dot of information. After he finished, he looked around for a plate but could not find one. He held the card and pencil in his hand, not knowing what to do with it. Just before they exited the church together, Sarah said, "You can drop the card in the labeled box next to the door." "Thank you," said Joshua," I was going to ask you what I should do with it." Joshua took the card and dropped it through the small slot of the wooden box labeled Guest Cards. He placed the pencil inside the holder attached to the box.

They walked out of the church onto the wooden walkway, with the sun up ahead, providing a beautiful day. The weather felt perfect, with streams of breezes blowing gently and children swaying around with the tide of joy accompanying the wind howling through the perfect day.

The kids ran around the grounds, chasing the flying butterflies without a care in the world. The church members headed towards their vehicles, which consisted majorly of pickups and wagons. Others stood around to speak with church members and to take a glimpse of the Mountain View before they departed.

"It was a wonderful sermon, wasn't it," said Sarah.

Joshua halted in his steps to reply to her. "Yes, the sermon was wonderful, and I must confess I was equally impressed by the band," he spoke eloquently. "What about you? What do you think about the band?"

"I loved the band," Sarah replied as they continued their walk.

"It was quite inspirational for me," Joshua added as they finally stepped off the wooden walkway and stepping on the grassy parking lot.

As they walked over to a car Sarah began stuffing her key into the lock while she temporarily split her attention between getting the door opened and talking to him; "You can ride with me," she offered. "You needn't worry about getting back; I'll drive you myself."

Joshua acknowledged her offer to assist him by walking to the other side of the car and letting himself in after she had unlocked the doors. The car was an old model, blue Chevrolet, but still adequate and pleasant looking to the eyes. They drove in silence for the next few minutes before she sought to break the silence with discussions about the church.

"What do you think of our church?" she began? "I mean the congregation itself and the entire setup."

"I loved the setting and the session itself," Joshua replied.

"Yes, it's an old church," Sarah chimed with her gaze on the road ahead of her.

"I know," Joshua spoke shortly. "I saw the sign outside the building before walking in."

The silence continued as they drove onto the highway before she broke the silence once more in a determined spirit to indulge him in a conversation.

"We have bible studies before church begins, I'd love you to come someday," she indulged him with a half-smile across her lips before taking her eyes back to the road. "It's only a small group, but we gather for breakfast at someone's house, and our hostess prepares the largest breakfast you've ever seen." Whatever item you desire for breakfast, She will have it. We all call it 'the all you can eat breakfast buffet.' I believe she wakes up at 5 am or so and cooks for all of us and she refuses to accept our help. "She is very generous," said Joshua. "We hope to raise enough money one day to build a larger facility, said Sarah."

Joshua listened with intent to her words, nodding in acknowledgment and smiling as they drove on. He enjoyed her company, and she liked the fact that he granted her listening ears.

"When we get a stable facility, we can build better classrooms, eating halls, theatre, and a gymnasium," she concluded, looking like a lady dreaming positively, which impressed Joshua.

"That would be a wonderful idea," Joshua noted, casting her a look before averting his gaze to the bicycle riders passing on the side of the road.

"I fancied the Pastor's sermon today, and I try never to miss any of his sermons because I always want to be a devoted and dedicated member of the church," she explained. "I adore the Lord with my heart, and cherish worshipping him."

"I'm very pleased to hear that," Joshua spoke with a mellow tone. He seemed like he meant every word he said. "The Lord and his Father will be overjoyed with how you pay close attention to them."

They had just driven off the highway and onto the town square road when he noticed the interconnecting wooden buildings and many people walking towards the buildings. The town reeked old, and y the information on a billboard they had passed, it was built in 1875.

"This used to be a trading post," she informed him. "You can find loads of tourists here at this time of the year coming to visit the Grand Tetons," she added, pulling her car onto an even rougher path than the one they were on before, which made the car bob up and down.

Joshua permitted himself some sightseeing, taking into view the houses and stores that had people moving in and out of them without care about being watched. They were used to having visitors around and had made it a point to live their lives normally as they should.

"What do the tourists get to do at the Grand Tetons?" he sought to know, looking at a family packed with their travel bags on their backs and holding some hiking equipment?

"They are the most important mountains in these parts and tourists go hiking and fishing as well as on hunt for some wildlife," she explained to the curious man who still looked outside the window.

"Oh, that explains the fishing equipment I saw earlier," he noted. "What do you do during the festive seasons around here?"

She looked at him like he was a curious cat, but one she was willing to indulge and enable him to have a wonderful time.

"When we have good snow, the tourists come to ski. During the

Christmas season we light up the town and turn the whole place to look like one big picture postcard," she shrugged. "We also go to the wilderness with the tourists included, to cut the largest tree we can find and place it in the middle of the town square."

Joshua could very much picture the entire thing already, and he knew he would love a taste of Christmas around there from the way she portrays the whole experience. Regarding what she talked about, his mind wandered far and well about the various occurrences.

"Do you simply place the tree there alone, or do you hang some fancy lights upon it?" he asked.

"Of course we light it up, as we do all the buildings as well," she shot him a fake frown. "We even hold a play about the birth of Jesus, by borrowing a baby from a local for an hour, while also having some live nativity scene with real live, docile animals people can pet.". "We have a donkey, a lamb, rabbits, and geese or two."

Joshua entertained himself with all of the information she had to offer, while she regaled him with descriptions of the various acts during the festive periods.

"Guess how we make the locals participate in the events and lending us a baby," she asked. "Come on and guess," she encouraged him.

Joshua spent the next few seconds without any answer, watching her face glow into one of frustration, but in a completely harmless way.

"We bribe them with gifts and presents when they participate," she answered her question just before driving towards a parking lot where there were lots of cars. The stores donate gifts from their stock all fully gift wrapped with ribbons and bows. The eateries give them gift cards to eat and drink whatever they want up to the card value.

"That's fascinating," he commended, as they eyed the lot for an available parking space. "What about that place?" Joshua pointed out on his right-hand side.

"That's perfect, someone is driving out," she noted, preparing herself to occupy the spot once the driver pulled out.

She parked the car perfectly into the comfortable spot with ample space for an exit, before turning off the engine.

"The café isn't far away from here, and we can walk to it," she assured him, getting out of the car first, while Joshua did the same thing.

They stepped out of the car and began to walk toward the café. While walking down the street, Joshua saw a $1 bill laying on the curb. He picked it up, and Sarah looked at him with an unexplained look. He wondered if she thought he was doing wrong until she spoke.

"It must be your lucky day," she congratulated him instead. A confused looking Joshua found himself asking, "Why?"

"I never find anything useful on the ground, not to mention money," she replied, watching Joshua do the most awkward thing by placing the cash back on the ground. "What exactly are you doing?"

"Some poor fellow must have dropped it," he said, staring at her. Perhaps he will come back and reclaim it.

"Nonsense, there is no name on it, how about you give it to the beggar up ahead?" she informed him, pointing towards a man not far from where they stood.

Joshua obliged, picking the cash back up and tucking it into his pocket before they got to the beggar. The beggar was partially blind, and his hazel colored eyes were glazed. He was old, and his skin wrinkled and dried by the parching sun. His clothes were ragged and unclean. His hair looked scruffy as he took off his hat and extended it outward. Others neglected him and walked by. He had been there the entire day, and no one had given him any money.

When Joshua came up to him, he extended his hat and said; "Can't you please help a poor man? I do not have any food and no home."

Joshua merely put his hand into his pocket and gave the man the 1 dollar bill he had found earlier. The beggar looked straight at Joshua, with his eyes widened, and his lips broadened into a smile.

"Thank you so much," he said happily. "Thank you very much and may God bless you," he continued.

"Thank you, sir" Joshua returned the kind words as they continued their walk towards the café.

Sarah looked at him with a smile, commending his gesture, even without further comment. As his eyes caught her smile, he felt the need to enlighten her;

"The poor in spirit are blessed, for the kingdom of heaven is theirs," he said. "I'm sure you've heard or learned of this from a church."

She nodded in acknowledgment. "I know and hope it will be true one day for everyone just as you said."

The beggar hadn't taken a proper look at the note Joshua had given to him and entertained the thought of how little the money could be of help to him since it was just a dollar. He felt partly disappointed because a dollar was not enough to buy him a cup of coffee or a decent meal. The beggar was grateful but was disappointed that he could have gotten more. Little did he know he was wrong. He took a proper look at the note he had in hand and realized that it was a hundred dollar bill and not just one dollar.

He stared at the bill again in confusion, swearing he had just been given a dollar bill and not a hundred dollar bill. He was sure that no one had come and changed it while he had it because it hadn't left his hand. He stretched out his arms into the sky and began giving thanks to God. He didn't care how loud his voice was, to the point his last cry in appreciation was loud enough to be heard by Joshua and Sarah.

"Thank you, Lord Jesus! Thank you" he yelled.

Sarah turned around immediately, casting a smile across her face before looking at Joshua.

"It seems you just made his day and made him happy at the same time," she shrugged.

"I like helping those in need sometimes," he responded with a smile accompanying his words.

～

They finally arrived at the café, which was a quaint one made of wooden logs. As they walked along the wooden walkway, they could see large out-door wooden decked patios enclosed in a small wooden fence. Along the fence line were plants of herbs and flowers, with herbs such as rosemary, thyme, sage, and mint while the flowers were daisies.

Sarah permitted herself a deep breath of air, taking into her lungs a full dose of the beautiful scent the flowers and various herbs provided into the air.

"The smell of those herbs and flowers are wonderful, aren't they?" she asked, seeking his opinion. She eyed him until he made a quick assessment personally by taking in a deep breath before responding.

"Yes, you're right, they're indeed wonderful," Joshua seconded her words. "I use a lot of herbs when I cook," said Sarah. "And may I ask what do you like to cook?" asked Joshua. "I like to make all kinds of vegetarian dishes." "I once was a meat eater but decided to go vegetarian," stated Sarah. "It is healthier for you, and I get so energized. I don't like it when they slaughter animals. They have feelings, you know. I will eat meat, only if nothing else is available and I have to survive. But even though if I have to, I will cry." "I sure understand how you feel, said Joshua." The Father gave manna to the Jews, but their desire for meat was too strong.

They stepped closer to the café, where they could see tables and chairs all made out of wood. Silverware, napkins, china, and glasses adorned the table. The air felt different within the café, and each of the tables had an umbrella providing shade from the sun or horrible weather while the diners ate.

Just by the wooden patio were a couple of magnificent oak trees that were mesmerizing to look at, and had a charming allure to them. Joshua took an extended look at them, admiring their every branch, limb, and leaf, and acknowledged the beauty they added to the environment.

"They're beautiful, aren't they?" she pointed out just behind him, jolting him back into consciousness. "I'm pretty glad they didn't cut them down while building the patio, else it would have been a waste of nature."

"I find fascinating how they built the patio around them," Joshua confessed.

As they approached the front door, Joshua saw a sign hanging on the post which read "Café Genevieve Inspired Home Cooking, 135 East Broadway," and another sign that had the word "Open" on it. Right next to the sign was a bike rack with some bicycles and a giant American flag hanging above them. The bicycles were speed bikes of every color, red, blue, white, yellow, purple, etc.

Joshua took his time to look at the bikes before assuming they belonged to people who came over to eat. His assumptions were right, with Sarah explaining just how far the distance was that people traveled from to dine at that particular café.

They finally walked into the café, where a hostess was waiting to welcome them in. The air had a pleasant smell to it. The aroma of delicious cooked food filled their nostrils. The entire room looked clean and spotless as evident from the air itself and the elegant tables all setup.

"Hello, and welcome to Café Genevieve, my name is Mandy," the attractive redhead with long hair and emerald green eyes welcomed them pleasantly.

She wore a blue jean and green shirt and held a couple of menus in her hand as she walked briskly to the empty table by the corner of the room to show them to their table. Sarah eyed her curiously, staring at the lady as she handed them the menu and went on ahead to briefly welcome a new set of people who had just walked in.

Joshua had noticed her lingering stare and nudged her out of it for it was rude.

"Sorry, you'd have to forgive me. The hostess reminds me of an old roommate I used to have. We used to fight over small things and eventually parted ways. I haven't seen her here before," she explained. "She must be new around here, I'm guessing."

"I had to draw your attention back," Joshua chuckled. "You were staring at her too long."

Mandy had just begun walking over to their table, while Sarah did her best to readjust and sit up. She wasn't going to give the wrong impression of herself to Joshua, or the hostess who had kindly helped them settle into a clean table.

"I'm sorry to keep you waiting, but a waitress will come to take your order soon," Mandy calmly recited like she had memorized the line over time and had gotten used to it.

Joshua started to make himself mindful of the interior of the Café. The lighting inside the restaurant was dim. The tables and chairs were made of solid wood and adorned with fine silverware, fine china, and thick drinking glasses. The floors were old and made of solid oak. The walls were painted green and decorated with framed paintings of fat pigs as well as a buffalo, bears, cows, and horses.

"I think they love pigs around here," Joshua pointed out, laughing playfully.

"You should try their Pig Candy, it's delicious," she proposed. "It is a salty, sugary slice of bacon." Sarah took the mason jar filled with thick slices of brown jerky laced with crushed paper and pushed it under his nose.

Joshua gave it some thought before deciding to decline; "I believe I'll pass on that." "I never was into sweet delicacies."

A fully stocked bar with the best variety of liquor was near the kitchen. They could see a couple of people sitting on the bar stools and talking to each other. One was having a cold beer and the other a glass of red wine.

Sarah eyed the glass of wine in the woman's hand. "Can it be a merlot, a Cabernet or a shiraz?" she said to herself. I feel like having a glass, but I am driving.

"I used to make wine," Joshua noted upon seeing her staring at their wine glass.

"Oh, really, what type of wine did you make exactly?" she asked. "My favorite is still Concord wine, but on occasions, I make a good Merlot."

Joshua looked startled by her talking about making wine.

"Do you know how to make wine too?" he asked, forgetting she had asked him first. "I'd like to try making wine someday because I really can't at the moment," she confessed. "My friends simply make a habit of taking me here, and we designate one of us that don't drink much so he or she will be the driver when we're heading back home." "Well, it isn't hard to get done once you know how to whip it up quickly," he told her.

Sarah scratched her chin in curiosity. "I heard it takes an awful lot of time to ferment and then age, how true is that?"

"It's pretty true, but there are ways to get it done more quickly than most people do," he piqued her interest with his words.

She leaned her head into a tilt, elbow on the table, and her wrist was correctly supporting her head which rested on it; "How do you get yours done more quickly than others?"

"Well, I can say I learned that from my father," Joshua replied immediately.

Sarah gently eased herself from resting on the table to peruse through the menu a bit. She surfed through the pages tirelessly, making funny faces and a somewhat indecisive one to tell Joshua just how much she was struggling with what to get or order. She finally caught his stare on her, bearing enough questions behind his eyes that he was speaking.

"Sorry, I actually know what's on the menu, but still make it a habit of finding it difficult to pick what I want every time I'm here," she explained to him. "Even though I know it very well, they have lots of delicious items on their menu and a wonderful chef whom I've known for quite some time."

Joshua accompanied her words with a nod.

"He's the best in the country," she stressed.'

Joshua had picked up his menu and began perusing the content too, with an equally worried look across his face. He studied them, and to him, it was like in a foreign language he hadn't seen before. He had just parted his lips to speak when he got interrupted by a waitress who had joined them.

She placed a small basket holding within it some bread, strawberry and grape jam and butter and two glasses of water on the table, while Joshua struggled on with his menu before laying it down. He looked across the table and stared at Sarah.

"I'm sorry, but I don't think I'll be able to afford anything on the menu," he sounded disappointed and a little ashamed. "I gave off the only dollar on me, and honestly have nothing else with which I could pay for the meal."

She shot him an angry look immediately, having asked him over to eat because she intended to pay the bill.

"Worry not, I'll take care of the bill, provided you pick reasonable food items within range," she finally smiled, letting off the frown on her face from earlier.

She could tell he was a tad bit embarrassed, so she stuck her gaze elsewhere to avoid getting him uncomfortable.

"I'm not hungry, so some bread and water will do," he informed her.

He hadn't thought it through before she spoke back immediately; "Really? Just bread and water?" she asked rhetorically, expecting no response from him. "How about the fact that man must not live on bread alone, but on every word that comes out from the mouth of God?" she grinned.

He couldn't help himself as she spoke. He had found her entire words amusing, in the context through which she had used them. He laughed hard and loud before calming himself to speak further.

"Since you put it that way, which in actuality is true, then I suppose some soup with my bread will do better than water," he shrugged.

Sarah waived to the waitress who had laid down the basket and kept her distance, just enough so they could converse, but not too far away, so she could be called upon when need be. She made her inquiries about the soup on the menu, before settling for a house salad with avocado and vinaigrette dressing. She ordered Joshua some onion soup after inquiring from him if he was okay with it.

They settled for some more water afterward, while declining the waiter's proposal for them to have some drinks. Joshua felt gladdened she had asked for water instead, without needing him to speak.

"Could you bring us some lemons and crackers with the order, please?" Sarah ordered finally, watching the waitress nod in acceptance, before turning around to leave.

The absence of the waitress provided some level of silence around the table which Sarah was quick to eradicate by pursuing some knowledge about a peculiar characteristic she had noticed on Joshua from the moment he had stepped into the church earlier.

She weighed the question thoroughly in her mind before finally letting it out.

"Can I ask you something?" she began with, watching Joshua's face get lit in curiosity.

"All right, you may go ahead," he encouraged her, sitting upright to answer her question with some enthusiasm brimming within him.

"Why do you walk with a cane?" she let it out without holding back.

Joshua looked uncomfortable to speak about his walk pattern but chose to indulge her nonetheless. She could read it from his demeanor and be going to ask him to forget she had asked when he regaled her with a brief sentence regarding her question.

With a soft sigh, he spoke; "I had a work-related incident, and sometimes, my legs give out which is why I need the support."

She could feel the pain laced around the words, making her uncomfortable that she had asked. Her face turned into a frown slowly, while she toyed with her fingers in desperate need to keep away from the topic.

"I'm sorry to hear that," she whispered underneath her breath in sympathy. "We have some church members who are handicapped and others in wheelchairs. They are mostly strong spirited people, and they accept the way they are."

"How do you think they came to accept their situation?" Joshua indulged her in helping her feel comfortable about the topic.

"It began with most of them accepting Christ and serving him, and things just worked out for them," she replied." "We also have someone at our church that is handicapped and visits their homes and consults with them to assist."

Joshua listened as attentively as he could, wearing a curious and fixated look on his face the entire time through. He couldn't help but feel some warmth from what Sarah was explaining to him. He included assisting the handicapped people in and around the church, build things around their homes, such as entry ramps for easy passage, and hinges on their doors, as well as carrying out chores they couldn't get done on their own, and running errands on a needed basis to make life comfortable for them.

"We have compassion for the handicap, yet we treat them like anyone else," she pointed out. "We don't ask anything in return to help them, and some become very actively involved in the Church." She smiled and continued. "For example one of our Church members named Gilbert, who became handicapped just a couple of years ago from a ski accident teaches an evening Bible class at the Church while being very good and inspirational."

"Wow, I must confess, what you guys do is nice," Joshua tendered in polite words.

She already felt drained from talking but did not want to stop without some questions to throw at him in the process.

"I'd like to know more about you?" she asked.

Joshua cast her a rhetorical look, aiming for her to state what her question was about accurately.

"I'm asking you to tell me some more about yourself, from where you're from, what you do, and the skills you might have," she straightened everything out for him.

Joshua couldn't help to show he had been pretty lost by her previous statement, with a nod to acknowledge he now understood her question.

"I was born and brought up in Israel, but my father asked me to come here," he briefly put his response to her. "I guess he intended for me to meet with people, get acquainted with the good ones and the bad ones, and see things in other parts of the world."

"Hmmm, you sound like a journeyman, but do you have a job?" she queried him further.

"I know how to build furniture, which I learned from my father," Joshua replied, willing to entertain her questions as best as he could. "It took some doing, but I'm pretty good at building things and anything, from a chair, a table, bookcases, to cabinets," he slightly boasted without meaning to do so.

She looked impressed, clapping her hands gently without making much sound in courtesy for those eating around them.

"Your father made a wise decision. I must say," she commended.

"America is a land of vast opportunities, and there's a mix of good and horrible people in it I must confess, even though there are times I feel the number of bad ones outweighs the good."

Joshua wore the same curious look Sarah had mostly on her face before she asked him a question. She could read that he had something to ask, and she waited patiently.

"What makes you think there are more bad people out there than good?" he finally let it out after a prolonged stare.

His face was flat in expression and bore nothing but a blank stare on it the entire time he spoke.

"As much as I feel there are loads of opportunities out there and everyone could have an honest living off them, most people are greedy, and they're most interested in themselves, and it makes it difficult for others to begin anything without having the money," she explained duly. "The greed is cancer in men, and it affects everyone struggling to make a living if you don't have some deep pockets to call upon."

"Oh, I see," he noted.

"I'd like to see some of your works though if I must be candid," she giggled interestingly. "That way, it would make it easier to recommend you to anyone who would be interested in making hand-made furniture."

"Of course, that would be lovely, and I'd love you to see them too," Joshua seconded her desire. "I would be pretty grateful."

"I overheard that our church's Pastor needs some additional pews, probably I could speak with him to hire you," she thought up a welcoming idea for Joshua. "The pay might not be much or what you'd need, since the church doesn't run on mighty income, but it should be good for a start."

Joshua looked happier than he had been before.

"That would be lovely, and whatever I can do for the church, would be strongly appreciated," he informed her with a smile.

"What about a place to stay?" Sarah popped up the one question she had been holding back in while she asked the rest.

Joshua briefly took a short look at her before answering "no." He didn't seem fazed by the fact that he had nowhere to sleep, and it bothered her a great deal.

"If no, then where do you sleep?" she adjusted in her seat to ask.

"I enjoy camping out and sleeping amongst the stars," he briefly replied.

His reply didn't sound good enough for her, with her lower jaw gently coming opened, and her eyes widening as he spoke.

"Please tell me you're joking," she wished that he was teasing her.

"It gets cold at night and what about the wild animals roaming around the wilderness? Aren't you scared of them?"

"No, not really, I adore and love them all," he spoke on the contrary to her belief. "Aren't they all beautiful?" She felt weakened by his response and perceived nonchalance towards being in danger sleeping outside and not having a place to stay and protect himself. She sighed hard and long, staring at the table as they waited for their food.

"How about I get you a bed, from a church member by the name Maggie?" she offered. "She owns a bed and breakfast place not too far away from the church. Perhaps I can request for her to let you stay there while you pay once you begin work."

Joshua could tell he wasn't going to win if he declined, and the prospect of getting a job would do just fine to pay up the rental fee.

"She's a pretty nice person, and a friend of mine, willing to help those in need," Sarah continued to sell him the idea of living with her friend.

He wasn't sure about the arrangement and the fact that he would be imposing.

"I'm sorry, but I don't think it's necessary, simply because I don't want to impose," he decided to decline.

Her face grew into a disheartened one, and her lips curled just into the perfect shape to let out her thoughts;

"Nonsense, I'll drive you there after our meal, but I have to leave early to meet with my mother who lives just a couple of hours from here." "You won't be imposing, and I need you to trust me."

Joshua felt convinced entirely, nodding his head to accept her offer, before seeking to know about her mother.

"She's not doing well," Sarah said. "She came down with leukemia, and my father alone is looking after her, and he's having a tough time because he has arthritis in one arm, and has just one arm to help her."

"I am so sorry to hear about that," Joshua sounded in sympathy.

The waitress brought out their food and placed it on the table while providing them with some napkins, some whole wheat crackers and a soup spoon for Joshua's soup. She put the large bowl of salad in front of Sarah before speaking.

"I put the salad dressing on the side," she said. "I wasn't entirely certain of how much you wanted."

Sarah took a quick look at the salad dressing, weighing the quantity to be just about enough; "Thank you, it's about enough."

"Would you care for anything else?" the waitress asked before she was to take her break. She looked from Joshua to Sarah intermittently, before providing ideas on some needs; "What about some hot sauce, peppers, pickles?"

Joshua waved his hands to indicate he needed nothing, while Sarah mirrored his actions politely.

"Thank you, but we're good, I believe," she said.

The waitress had just left when Joshua bowed his head, with his eyes closed, and his hands extended towards Sarah's.

"Let's say a prayer," he noted, feeling her hands get tucked into his, while she bowed her head as well.

Sarah took the impetus to pray;

"*Heavenly Father, we thank you very much for giving us this nourishment so that it will fuel our bodies and give us the strength to worship you every day. Please bless Joshua and hope that our congregation accepts him and that he finds work so that he can support himself and your church in the holy name Amen.*"

They let go of each other's hands and settled to dig into their food with no words said. They spent the first few minutes slowly nipping away at their meals before Sarah ventured toward trying to know Joshua better. He hadn't anything else to do, and her company was more than pleasant, so he chose to indulge her.

He spoke at length about his childhood, and family, while she shared her attention in between her meal and his stories. Joshua spoke well of his father, mother, brothers, and sisters through the course of the meal, which held some extraordinary amount of fascination in the tales he told, to Sarah.

She shared her family tales with him as well, hitting it off into a pleasant conversation with him as they consumed their meal to its end. Joshua had enjoyed every bit of the soup and their discussion, wiping his mouth clean with the napkin the waitress had provided, while Sarah did the same.

They had just gotten through when the waitress showed up again.

"How was your meal?" she initially asked.

"It was wonderful, thank you," Joshua politely responded. He had spoken for both of them, and it was well understood.

"I'm glad you enjoyed your meals, but would you be interested in having a piece of our homemade peach cobbler or a cup of coffee to compliment the meal you had?" she smiled as she asked with her hands behind her back.

Sarah declined her offer politely, while Joshua did the same, citing the reason to be the need to watch his weight. His words had prompted some laugh from Sarah, who couldn't figure out what he intended to watch in his excellent frame.

"Here is your bill," the waitress set the paper on the table for Sarah who picked it up in one hand and began to review the charges as if she was an auditor reviewing an expense report. "I need to figure out a good tip for the waitress," said Sarah. "I like to leave a handsome tip when someone treats me right." "Sounds justifiable," said Joshua.

She had just held the bill in her hand when someone snatched it from her in a quite rapidly manner, as she turned around to hear the familiar voice of someone she couldn't mistake for anyone else. It was a lady, and one Sarah couldn't help but smile about when she spoke. She was a tall, thin, witty, and mature woman. Her skin was tanned, her hair chestnut color and shoulder-length. She wore frameless glasses, and her eyes were dark brown. She wore light lip gloss.

"I prohibit you from taking care of this bill today," she said, grinning as Sarah made eye contact with her finally. "You assisted me in getting a good electrician, and I believe I'm in debt to you."

"You don't need to do that," Sarah tried talking her out of it by raising her hand in an attempt to get the bill, but the lady declined.

"No, I must insist," she insisted. "You need to see the great job your electrician did updating the lighting system outside our restaurant. Before I met him, I got screwed by a guy named Oslo, who practically didn't know what he was doing," she explained.

Joshua listened on while Sarah looked back at him before turning her attention to the lady again. She wanted her bill back, but with each passing second, it seemed more like an impossible task.

"When I tried turning off the lights inside the café back then, the lights with the light sensors outside went off," she lamented further about her predicament before Sarah assisted her with a better electrician.

"I'm glad I could be of help," Sarah spoke. "Berry is a member of our church and an excellent electrician."

She had just ended her sentence when she caught the woman's eyes over Joshua, knowing it was the first time she had seen him there and intended an introduction to be made.

"Pardon my manners," Sarah briefly apologized. "Joshua, I want you to meet Jamie, the manager in charge here, and Jamie, meet Joshua, a friend of mine," she introduced, watching the two adults exchange a brief handshake.

"It's nice to meet you, Joshua," Jamie said, before turning to Sarah. "So, how are you doing dear?"

Sarah ran her fingers through her hair before speaking; "I'm fine, but mom isn't," she stated...

"What's going on with her?" Jamie extended a heart of concern.

"She got diagnosed with cancer, and it's been tough on her," Sarah recounted the horrifying experience. "I'll be seeing her soon, though, to know how things are with her."

"I'm so sorry to hear that," Jamie sympathized. "I, for one, know how difficult it can be with cancer."

"Yes, she might have to get chemo, depending on what the doctor orders," Sarah noted.

The air around them had turned into a gloomy one with the talk of sickness. Joshua kept to himself, choosing not to interfere in their discussion or be rude in any way.

Jamie sighed gently, before wearing a frown; "I hope the drugs work," she said, laying her hand to rest on Sarah's shoulder. "I hope so too, and in due time because it's causing a strain on dad while trying to take care of her with his condition," she bellowed. "With them living so far away and out of town, it has become even more difficult to assist them."

"You never know dear, but God allows us to be tested for our faith in different ways to see how much we can persevere," Jamie put it to her. "Just keep strong and be faithful, and all will turn out well."

Sarah acknowledged her words with a nod.

"It's running late, and we need to be on our way," she got up saying.

Jamie gave her a warm hug, engulfing her into her arms before whispering aloud; "I hope to see you again soon."

"Thank you very much," Sarah said, before watching Jamie turn around to Joshua.

"You take care of this one," she said with a wink. "You got yourself an excellent catch," she added with a giggle.

~

Sarah and Joshua left the café and walked back to their car. They drove away from the town and headed out to Maggie's "Bed and Breakfast" which was on the outskirt of town, overlooking the mountains and the lake.

They had just driven past the mountains, when Sarah pointed out the beautiful scenery the mountains provided, which Joshua was more than willing to acknowledge.

"I could never live anywhere else," Sarah chimed behind the wheel. "My mother had me in her house, choosing not to give birth in the hospital, and it freaked my father out," she laughed.

"That's an odd choice, but was your father able to manage with it?" Joshua enjoined in the conversation.

"No, he wasn't, but he said he prayed his heart out through the entire process for no complications," she replied. "Gladly, there was nothing of such, and I came out healthy."

"He has so much faith and delighted to know," Joshua noted.

"Yes, he does, and he is a true believer in Christ," she added, pulling out of the main road onto one that branched off from it.

They drove down a gravel road and past a sign with an arrow indicating "Maggie's Bed and Breakfast." She approached the "Bed and Breakfast," stopped the car in front of the house and began to honk the horn.

Maggie, a middle-aged black woman, with well-tanned smooth skin and long curly frizzled black hair came running out upon hearing the honk of the horn. She wore large silver hoop earrings, and she wore a long light blue dress with a large turquoise necklace. She was a woman with a heart of gold, a believer in Christ and very active in the Church.

Sarah stepped out of the car quickly and ran up to Maggie with open arms. She was happy to see her. She hugged her and gave her a gentle kiss on the cheek.

"How are you doing Maggie?" Sarah asked. "You look well," she added.

Joshua had just walked up to them when Maggie spoke.

"Oh yes, the weather has been lovely this past week, and above all asides taking advantage of it," she giggled.

Sarah stretched her hand toward Joshua, asking him to come over;

"Maggie, let me introduce you to a friend of mine," she began. "Maggie, meet Joshua, who just came into town and needs a place to stay" "Joshua, I want you to meet Maggie, the lady I was telling you about."

Maggie shook Joshua's hand, feeling it firmly in a grip, unlike any he had thought from a woman. He stared at her with a smile, before nodding in respect. She smiled back at him before turning to Sarah.

"It's always nice to meet someone new," she smiled. "Why don't you both come on inside and get out of the cold," she insisted, leading the way into the house.

They followed Maggie inside the home. It was a quaint little home furnished with antiques. On the walls, she had religious oil paintings such as Christ on the cross and Christ on the donkey, depicting his triumphal entry into Jerusalem and on the floor, brass floor lamps. Facing one wall was just an upright piano and a wooden bench. The keys looked to be an antique and were a bit worn out. On the keyboard were Christian lyric sheets which looked rumpled from many users.

Knickknacks cluttered the room. On the end of the room, there was a wall of shelves, with old looking books of various sizes and shapes. The sight of books attracted Joshua, who walked over gently to it in a bid to find out what kind of books they were. They were old and dusty, but still pretty much readable with some good cleaning and dusting.

Some had their hinges torn and pages missing, but a more significant proportion remained intact, albeit some in great difficulty.

"Are you interested in books, Joshua?" Maggie asked from across the room. "If so, we have a lot of Christian books which you can read and some videos too," she informed him.

"Do they belong to anyone in particular?" Joshua was forced to ask, knowing it could be someone's property, and he wouldn't want to impose or be rude without the owner's permission.

"No, they are there for guests who are interested in reading them," Maggie answered him. "You're more than welcome to read any of the books and check them out as much as you like or fancy."

Joshua felt glad at heart as he swept his eyes around the library in front of him. He took into account the various colors of the books and their well-arranged manner, before extending his hand carefully towards the shelf to take out a book from it. It was a brown leather bound book. The edges of the pages were embossed with gold as well as on the front cover, with the title "The Torah both in Hebrew and English."

He stared at it intensely for some seconds, paying no attention to anything or anyone else in the room the entire time. Gently, he rubbed his hand over the cover, noting it had been kept clean enough by whoever did the dusting, which he could guess must be Maggie, before gently raising it to his lips to kiss the book.

He opened the book, which contained within it, the five books of Moses as its content. He thumbed through the pages to the Chapter of Leviticus and browsed over the Laws that his father had set. He had just noticed Maggie was still staring at him when he raised the book high enough for her to see.

"I like reading this one," he said atop his voice, before letting his hand down.

Maggie smiled back at him, indicating she fancied his choice of a book with a nod accompanying her gesture.

"You're most welcome dear," she eased in words from where she stood before casting her gaze away from him momentarily.

Joshua flipped through the pages one after the other, familiarizing himself with the words he knew by heart already, but still enjoyed every opportunity to reread them. His eyes were stern in focus, and his hands held the book like it was life itself and delicate in feel. He hadn't taken note of Maggie and Sarah speaking as he engulfed himself with the material in his hand until Maggie's loud call alerted him of his needed attention.

"Please come with me, let me show you to your room," she beckoned on the man whose interest in the book he held fascinated her dearly.

He obeyed, slapping the book closed gently, before walking over to where the two lovely ladies stood.

"I'll be here early enough tomorrow to meet with the Pastor as we discussed earlier," Sarah informed him with a hint of haste in her tone.

He could tell she was barely keeping strong and trying not to show how badly she needed to be by her ailing mother. He respected and fancied the fact she cared much for her parents, adding to the list of beautiful qualities he had noted in her since they met at the church.

He nodded to show he had heard her loud and clear, with no further words to say in hopes of delaying her no further, as Sarah took the queue and jetted out the door. He watched her back move a distance from them, before turning back to Maggie. Patiently she was waiting for him to get through.

"Shall we?" he asked like a gentleman with an outstretched arm.

"Yes, we shall Joshua, come let me show you to the room you'll be staying in," she responded with a chuckle.

He followed behind her like a puppy attached to its mother, treading carefully on the creaking floorboards, and taking note of the establishment in its entirety, which looked old, but very much well maintained. They finally arrived at his room, with Maggie walking in first. She had picked up some freshly laid towels from the hallway closet earlier, to put them on the bed.

She stood aside, watching him drop his backpack on the floor just by the bed stand and not entirely far away from the wall. He had only intended turning his back away from the bag when the sight of something shining from the floor caught his gaze. It looked no more than three inches long, and an inch wide in size.

He bent over to pick it up, taking the strange object into his hand and taking a good observation of it as he stood there. It was a fascinating piece. On the top was a gold crown and on the bottom, a handle like you find on a small scroll that was also gold. The object was tubular and had hammered impressions. The color was a light blue and on the main body was a raised embossed gold symbol in the form of a "W" which was familiar and equally surprising.

"Isn't that Hebrew?" he thought to himself, looking at the markings to be sure.

Maggie had neared him to have a glimpse of the object as well.

"This is a Mezuzah if I'm not mistaken?" Joshua showed it to her, asking. "I'm quite surprised by what it would be doing on the floor in the room," he noted.

He gently asked her to hold out her hand and eased the object into her right palm, where she could have a better look at it. She admired it entirely, sharing in his thoughts and wondering what it was indeed doing in the room on the floor. They said nothing to each other for the next few seconds, before Maggie finally looked up at him.

"This is strange, I must confess," she noted. "I'm pretty certain it was nailed down on the front of the door to your room and would normally take a crowbar to pry it out should you ever intend to."

Joshua looked to the door, seconding her thoughts in his reasoning. It was impossible for the object to have found its way down from the door without some practical assistance from a prying bar or object.

"Do you have any suggestions regarding how it might have gotten there?" Joshua asked her.

Maggie nodded with her eyes staring at her clenched hand; "The previous owners of this establishment were Jews and had a whole lot of such paraphernalia hanging around the walls and rooms entirely."

"So they must be the ones who had taken it down when they sold the place?" Joshua suggested.

"No, I wouldn't say so, because I have always seen it hanging on the door post, but the previous guests might be responsible for what I can remember," she corrected him. "They were a curious bunch and might have thought about taking it as a memento as a piece of good luck charm to ward away evil spirits."

Joshua rubbed his chin upon her explanation, drawing some better understanding from all she had just said. He had his impressions set, and he was going to share it with her. He extended his hand to have it back on his palm before explaining.

"It all makes sense," he said.

"What?" Maggie asked.

"The reason the past guests might have thought about taking it for themselves," he pointed out. "There are those who believe it helps keep away evil spirits as you said, but that is not true. Inside the

Mezuzah, you will find two chapters from the Torah, written in Hebrew," he granted her a better understanding of his thoughts.

Maggie looked like she was learning of it for the first time. Her eyes narrowed into focus on the piece of the object in his hand, while her hands stood akimbo on her hips.

"The essence of the Mezuzah is the concept of Oneness of God," he continued. Lifting the object high enough for her to look at properly; "The very first verse written on the Mezuzah is the Shema, which states... ."

"*Listen, Israel! The Lord our God, the Lord is One.*"

"The second verse reads... '*Love the Lord your God with all your heart, with all your soul, with all your strength and write them on the doorpost of your house and on your gates.*"

His knowledge of things baffled and amazed her at the same time. His eloquence was nothing like she had seen before, and she admired it sincerely.

"The written payer inside should not be printed mechanically but painstakingly by hand," he was about continuing when she interrupted him.

"Joshua, I need to speak with Sarah briefly, and breakfast comes as early as 8 a.m., but in case you need anything, please inform me," she politely excused herself from his sight.

"Thank you," Joshua responded as she stepped out of the room and left him nothing but her absence.

He helped himself onto the bed, with his back against it, and his face was staring at the ceiling, which was of drab color but neat and well kept without spider webs and dust. He could feel Maggie hadn't entirely gone, and her eyes stared at him with high intensity, as she helped the door to a close.

He could feel nothing but silence in the room, as he turned and tossed, with his head placed on the pillow. The antique glass chandelier on the ceiling provided him something to look at, as he entertained himself briefly by admiring it until it could no longer tickle the fancy of his admiration.

The bright light shining through the crystals hit his eyes and made him cast his gaze away after staring at it for far too long. The bed felt comfortable enough for him to realize just how tired he was beginning to get. He had had a pretty tiring day, and his body needed some rest to recuperate his strength before morning would come.

He had just begun dozing off when he heard a sound as if a bird was rustling its wings. He opens his eyes halfway. An angel appeared at the foot of his bed. He had a pretty good view of the angel from the corner of his eyes as he watched the angel without getting up from his sleeping position.

The gigantic figure almost as tall, with broadened wings; large enough to swallow no less than five people as he expanded them from the ceiling to the floor, made him a beautiful sight to gaze.

His clothes were snowy white and smoky, and he had a stern look directed right at Joshua, who remained in bed without moving a muscle. It was his duty to watch over Joshua, and he was sure to do it as best as he could with nothing permitted to stand in his way. "Is it Gabriel or Uriel," he said.

The silence in the room lingered on, just before Joshua opened his eyes fully to the sound of cutleries in the kitchen, the angel disappeared. He had thought Sarah was gone, but he was wrong.

~

Maggie had just gotten a silver tray from the kitchen and a variety of assorted cookies for Sarah, before returning with them. She laid them before the tired looking lady with a smile across her face. "I know you must be tired honey you look exhausted," she pointed out correctly. "This is why I got you some coffee and cookies to help replenish your spent energy." "I have your favorite." Oatmeal raisin, chocolate chip chunks with pecans, and some sugar cinnamon.

Sarah welcomed her generosity with a weak smile.

"I would have loved to sit with you and have them, but the caffeine in the coffee makes me jittery," she replied honestly. "I'm also short on time, and I need to see my mother pretty soon, Maggie, she came down with Leukemia and just had chemo-therapy from what the Dr. told me."

Maggie frowned with concern. She hadn't any idea she was battling such hurt underneath. "I'm so sorry to hear about your mom."

"I don't know what to do," Sarah confessed in more painful words. "Dad has been taking care of her, but it's taking its toll on him, and you know he has arthritis."

She needed to speak no more, as Maggie helped herself up from her seat. She wrapped her warm body and hands around her friend in a show of support and love for her. She had nothing to offer other than her support through prayers and faith.

"You need to have faith dear, and believe God will help you and your family through this," she advised. "I can assure you everything will be okay," she added, helping her friend wipe some beads of tears sliding down her cheeks.

She nodded tenderly and profusely. She believed every word Maggie had told her, and she said herself within that all she needed was to pray hard to God and find in him without any form of a condition attached to it. She took a moment to mull through her pain before casting it aside with faith in her heart that all would be well. She intended to pray some more about it later on.

"I have a favor to ask of you, Maggie," she informed her friend.

"Come on out with it honey, what do you need?" Maggie encouraged her to go on.

Sarah shifted uncomfortably in her seat, staring her in the eyes with a hint of hold back in her voice before she decided upon letting it out boldly.

"Joshua has no money on him at the moment, but he builds furniture, and I'm going to ask the Pastor if he can hire him to make the new pews for the Church," she explained while Maggie listened on. "Can he pay you when he gets paid, please?"

Maggie sighed deeply, chuckling afterward like she had thought it was a grave matter Sarah wanted to ask about as a favor. Her smile informed Sarah of her intent already before she even spoke.

"I can assure you that's no problem, Sarah," she planted her hand on her friend's shoulder saying. "I'm always here to help anyone in need, and you know that."

Sarah felt pretty glad, sighing in relief, and let out a heart-warming smile afterward.

"Perhaps he could build me that rocking chair with a glass holder which I've always wanted," she giggled gladly. "I can see myself sitting out on the porch with my lemonade in hand and drinking it as I so please," she giggled some more.

Sarah couldn't help but smile at her gesture.

"I'm sure he would be more than willing to get it done for you," Sarah assured her before glancing at her watch.

Night had fallen upon them, and the darkness was thickening with each passing minute.

"It is getting late, and I better go, but I'll stop by tomorrow evening to pick him up," Sarah eased herself out of the chair in excuse, picking up one of the cookies in respect for Maggie's troubles. "Thanks for this by the way."

Maggie gladly appreciated her gesture with a "Thank you" in return. Sarah had just walked to the door when she called out to her; "Be careful out there honey, I hear there's a storm brewing around somewhere not far away!"

Sarah didn't turn around before replying; "I sure will," then she hurriedly headed off to her car and drove off.

Maggie closed the door behind her gently, before returning to the delicious cookies on the table waiting for her to help herself.

CHAPTER 3

S arah's Accident
That early morning Sarah began her journey to see her mother and father. She had been driving for the past half hour in silence, but with a burdened mind. Sarah could feel pangs of hurt lurk around in her heart, while her mind drowned in worries about the state her mother was in and how much suffering her father had to endure. The drive was more prolonged and lonelier than she could recall it usually was.

The absence of someone to talk to through the drive made it worse, while within she could feel Joshua's lack the entire time through. She decided to feed and fuel her mind with other things and thoughts, with the beautiful sight of the mountains' snow caps coming to mind. She stared at them with longevity and tried escaping from the inner turmoil her heart held.

Flanking her on the road, were a couple of deer feeding on the green pastures nature had provided for them freely, amidst thoughts of what Joshua had told her about God being a creative designer and a talented one to create such beautiful creatures as he saw fit. She could still picture how he had said it with so much conviction and certainty that she couldn't help but smile.

"You're right," she muttered within the comfort of her car.

With a sigh and desire to feed herself with better emotions, she began humming one of the songs she had sung through in church earlier. She looked out the car through the front glass, staring at the sky, which had begun gathering clouds in a show of incoming rain, sooner than later. She had forgotten about the storm Maggie had warned her about until the thought came running through the beds of her mind again.

The air had begun getting colder, and as she looked up, she noticed that the sky was getting cloudier. She shivered gently within the comfort of her car, feeling the cold make a quick rattle of her entire body. She reached for the heater within her car, turning it on and allowing the warmth to help chase away the cold that had quickly spread around her body.

She reached out her right hand to the vent to warm it up, while the left simultaneously kept on driving, trying her best to keep as warm as possible and not catch a cold.

"I wish it were summer," she sighed, feeling her hand get the needed warmth she sought.

The sky had begun dropping snowflakes on her windshield, prompting her to turn on her windshield wipers, while she watched the wipers get their job done as she drove on. She had driven further up the road when the horizon came into focus just up ahead. She could see a sizable concrete underpass, the only one built to connect the freeway to that part of the interstate.

Approaching the underpass, she could make out the image of an eighteen-wheeler flatbed truck crossing. The truck was hauling rolls of chain link fence poorly layered above each other to prevent them from falling off. She fixed her eyes on the rolls. "I remember buying chain link fence for the Church's October pumpkin patch event," she said. "Each roll on that truck must be 6 Ft x50 Ft long and weight approximately 130 lbs. or so," she murmured.

The truck moved fast, paying little attention to the safety of the goods it carried, before the sudden, ear piercing, screeching sound of the brakes from the truck alerted Sarah to the dangerous swerve of which had just lost control. It had come unexpectedly and fast without any prior signs of what was to come.

Sarah felt her eyes blink fast, capturing the danger coming her way.

"Crap! There must be ice on the road," she thought to herself. She had just neared the underpass when the truck which had struggled to gain control before she got close enough, had begun losing its load and bundles of chain link fence, which started to dropping dangerously from above unto the road beneath.

Sarah swerved to the right and managed to dodge the rolls of chain link fence while trying to avoid being struck by the incoming bundles from the other side as well. She maneuvered the car as best as she could, feeling her legs work hard to kick on the pedal, while her hand worked the gear simultaneously. She moved as best as she could, feeling her heart begin to race violently, while her eyes narrowed in focus.

Adrenalin pumped through her veins at a tremendous rate while her hands tightened on the steering wheel. She could barely do enough, just before a bundle fell right in front of the car and sent the vehicle into a jolt. The resulting swerve placed the vehicle in the perfect position to receive another bunch of fencing that landed onto its windshield, cracking it immediately.

Her car swerved out of control instantly, running out of the road in the process. Her tire hit a small boulder on the side of the road, sending the car into the air in a dangerous flight pattern before it came back landing on the ground and continuing in a spiral tumble down the side of the pastured road. She could feel herself get smashed and rammed against the inside of her car, before being tossed out of the wholly shattered windshield.

The levitation came with great pain, before the final smash against the ground, where the movement became impossible to carry out, and she knew things weren't right within her. Her face looked towards the sky while remaining still with her vision becoming hazy, while blood trickled from her head, down her forehead, and onto her lips.

She felt the jolts of pain shoot around her body in a vast sum, while her limbs felt numb and helpless in the process. She slightly opened her eyes, and all she could see was a haze and the rays of the sun. She closes her eyes and re-opened them, just as a figure came hovering over her. She straightened her sight, is the only muscle she had control over, trying her best to see, as to her surprise, the image began to morph into one of Joshua.

She could see his mouth move, but the words weren't permeating her ears as they should. She strained to hear what he was saying, as he knelt closer to her with his hand on his knee.

"Hey, Sarah, it's me, Joshua. You just had an accident, but you'll be fine, someone will rescue you" he spoke in such a calm tone that she believed him, but still felt surprised that he had shown up. "Don't try to move before the ambulance gets here to get you to the hospital."

She struggled to keep awake but found it difficult. Her eyes closed gently, before coming open again to see Joshua had vanished out of her sight. She couldn't comprehend what was going on but could swear she had seen him right there just a few seconds past. She could feel it within her too.

The blazing sound from an ambulance's siren alerted her of their presence, she gently closed her eyes, while a medic jumped out the back of the ambulance and began running toward her. She could feel their existence, but her mind had drifted off as the pain finally came to a stop. All that was going on around her became unknown, as the visions faded, and she closed her eyes.

"Hurry up, we don't want to lose her," a medic told his colleagues as they carried out the operation of taking her vitals. In a boisterous voice, the medic called out to Sarah. "Hello, what's your name? I need you to stay with me, so please, tell me your name."

They needed to keep her awake, with the fear she might fall off to sleep and not wake up again.

One of the medics found her purse just a few feet away from the car. The medic opened her bag and pulled out her ID. She read the name out, "Sarah Abrams."

"We better get her to the hospital right away," she hurried her colleague. "She suffered a concussion and possibly broke her neck."

They helped put a neck brace on her immediately, before gently picking her up to place her on the mobile cart before lifting her into the back of the ambulance. They drove off in a hurry to the nearest hospital, after ascertaining she was the only one in the car.

CHAPTER 4

M*iracles of Healing at the Hospital*
Upon their arrival at the hospital, Sarah was wheeled into the intensive care unit to begin work on reviving her and dealing with the injuries she has sustained.

They called her parents immediately without delay, to make them aware of the tragic accident. Sarah's parents were deeply disturbed to hear the news, and they were worried that her father decided to call the Pastor immediately without delay.

It had taken no less than half an hour after the first call took place when the Pastor got patched through on his call to the doctor in charge of Sarah's case. He sounded calm, and more composed, unlike Sarah's father, who was jittery and sounded like a man mentally and emotionally paralyzed as he narrated the current ordeal to the Pastor.

"Hello doctor, I'm calling to ask about a lady by the name Sarah Abrams," her Pastor spoke through the phone.

"Hello. I'm Dr. Walker, and I'm glad to hear from you, sir, but her condition is quite critical," the doctor explained. "She was in a car accident, with a concussion and some injuries, but we're working towards making certain she's stable at the moment."

He could hear the man on the other end of the line sounding worried.

"We've just done an x-ray, and we'll ascertain other injuries within a moment, but you can rest assured we will do our best," the doctor tried his best assuring him.

The same hours of the night, her Pastor called as many church members as he could, asking for the news to be disseminated about Sarah's car accident. He asked that they begin to pray for her life, and reach out as best as they could to her.

Maggie was the last person to be notified; she had fallen asleep when a persistent call came in continuously without count. Hearing about Sarah's accident sent a terrible stream of pain immediately down her spine. She couldn't fathom how and why such a thing had happened to her after they had just seen each other a few hours back.

Maggie had been so desperate to head out irrespective of the storm brewing to see Sarah but was informed of Sarah's condition that she would be in intensive care and that no visitors were allowed. She was determined to be the first at the hospital the following morning, though. She took her time to think about it but still could not remain at home without being around Sarah.

She walked to the door of the one companion she had, and the man she was sure would need to know of his friend's state.

Joshua was not sleeping. He was reading the bible and was startled when he heard the loud, rapid knock on the door, and his eyes became wide open. Joshua jumped out of bed like a grasshopper hurling across the room. He walked to the door to open it, while

Maggie's frame stood right in front of him, looking worried, sick and jittery.

"What's going on, Maggie?" he asked, waiting for her to let him in on the situation of things?

"It's about... about Sarah," she tried hard to speak but found it difficult. "She just got involved in an accident while driving and has been admitted into intensive care."

Joshua's face wore a sad expression immediately. She could see the hurt apparent from his gaze.

"Will you please accompany me to the hospital tomorrow?" she beckoned on him.

He didn't wait for her to end her words properly before answering; "Yes, I will, and I'll be praying for her soul as well."

Maggie returned to her room, quietly stepping down the hallway until she was out of sight. Joshua had waited for her to leave, before closing his door and heading towards the window. He spread apart the window curtains, revealing the beautiful sky with millions of stars shining brightly in it up above. He knew what he had to do, and it was the only thing he could.

He kneeled and looked outside the windows. The cold howling wind rushed into his room and smashed against his face. He closed his eyes, with his hands held together, while his lips began to move fervently. He began to pray as hard as he could.

He prayed for Sarah.

He found it relieving that she was a believer, and knew there would be others praying for her as he did too.

"My prayer isn't for Sarah alone, but for those who will harken unto me in faith through this message," he said to himself.

He went ahead to pray for the next three hours without ceasing.

It was the only way he knew to get things done, and he would do it no other way.

~

Morning finally came after the restless night. Joshua came down from his room to the breakfast table with no hint of worry in his demeanor or eyes. Maggie eyed him as he approached until he stopped before her with a smile.

"Good morning, Maggie, how did you sleep?" he greeted, still with no hint that something horrible had happened to her friend.

"I didn't sleep much," Maggie replied.

"Is it because of Sarah's accident?" Joshua asked the obvious question.

"Yes, I feel so worried about her," Maggie chimed with a hurting tone.

"I was worried about her too, but she will be okay, and we'll meet with her after breakfast," Joshua assured her in his calm state.

His countenance got her somewhat uncomfortable and baffled, but she wasn't going to hold it against him. She had hoped to skip breakfast, too, but she had some visitors she couldn't help but feed in proper courtesy. She set about whipping some quick batches of pancakes, scrambled eggs, and turkey sausage. She lay the maple syrup on the table and also put a large bowl of fruits with it.

Maggie also made hot tea and coffee and served the guests their breakfast, while Joshua sat down at the table and introduced himself to a couple and a gentleman. The couple had just gotten married, and Joshua congratulated them with blessings. They present themselves as Howard and Sandra. Howard was a man in his mid 50's, medium height and weight. He was slightly bald and combed his dark brown hair back to cover a thin patch. He wore thick black framed glasses and sported a V-neck sweater and blue jeans. Sandra, on the other hand, was quite the opposite. She was in her mid 40's and medium height, slim, with brown eyes, and fair skin. Her long dark hair cascaded down her back. She wore a flower pattern pastel dress.

"How long have you been married, Howard?" Joshua asked, staring at the blooming wife, who looked radiant and didn't want to let go of her husband's hand.

"We've been married three weeks now, and we came here for our honeymoon, hoping to settle here as well," he responded, before kissing his wife passionately.

"I can assure you both, that there is no better place to settle than here," he enticed them with the prospect further. "We also have a wonderful church you could attend around here, if you're Christians, though."

The wife smiled. My Father was an evangelist. We come from a Christian home."

"What about you, Howard, are you a Christian too?" Joshua queried.

The man took a brief look at his wife before replying in a nervy manner; "Well, I was born Jewish with both my parents born into Jewish homes, but I've never been into a church before," he confessed.

"Well, when the time comes, we will see we have but one.

God and all religions will be made whole in due time," Joshua spoke to him, before turning to the other man in the room.

"Hello, my name is Joshua, and what is your name"? "My name is Patrick. You can call me Pat". Pat was a businessman going through some form of crisis by the way he sighed intermittently and kept barking into his phone in anger. He had a scruffy looking plaid suit on, which looked like he had slept in it, while bags were underneath his eyes. His hair was white, and he was medium height, slightly overweight with a bulging belly, pale skin and brown-red hair.

"What about you, sir, are you willing to move into the area?" Joshua indulged him.

The man looked up with a disheartened look still masking his face.

"I don't think so," he spoke bitterly.

Joshua could tell there were things troubling his heart.

"I just had a nervous breakdown and decided on having a sabbatical to help get me better, and still don't know if there is anything I'm interested in doing for now and it's pretty frustrating," he continued.

He watched the man sulk some more before lending a piece of advice. "There are times things happen for reasons we are unable to see or fathom, and in such cases, it could be God trying to put you to test for a better life ahead, provided you trust in him and remain patient."

Joshua extended his hand to touch Pat's shoulder, comforting him with the words; "God always asks us to come to him and lay our burdens upon him."

Pat nodded his head, with an accompanying sigh, before trying his best to lighten up with a grin.

Maggie had just arrived shortly to inform them of their trip to the hospital for a dear friend who got involved in a car accident. She asked them to leave the dishes on the table for her, which would be tended to when she got back without delay, before heading out the door.

Joshua followed behind her hurriedly, trying to keep in pace with her. They got into her black minivan and drove off to the hospital. Maggie could barely hold herself as they pulled into the road. He had been watching her the entire time to make sure she was fine, but clearly, she could not be.

She looked at him with tears flooding her eyes; "I'm worried sick about her," she confessed.

"I can assure you she'll be okay and remains within the glorious hands of the Lord," he sympathized with her.

Maggie sucked in her tears loudly.

"I still can't believe or understand why this happened to her while she was on her way to see her parents," she sighed. "It shouldn't happen to someone like her."

Joshua didn't believe in her last statements and knew such occurrences had their reasons.

"There are reasons these sorts of things happen, and at times, Satan has a role to play in such evil acts," Joshua lent his view.

"I wish the world could be free of that evil," Maggie fumed. "I imagine a world where he would just cease to exist."

"That would come to be soon, Maggie," Joshua chuckled slightly.

∾

They drove for the next few minutes in silence, before arriving at the hospital. It was a large one, with people driving into the parking lot, and bodies walking in and out the front door. The sight of the massive structure struck a chord of nervousness within Maggie as she brought the car to a halt. She wasn't one for hospitals and avoided them as best as she could.

Joshua could see her anxiety, but left her to deal with it alone, knowing people had to overcome their demons at times through sheer will and personal decision. They got out of the car, walking side by side after Maggie press her remote and lock her car up.

They walked through the front door, to the pungent smell of drugs and other cleansing agents the hospital used regularly. They walked briskly, past injured men and women with bandages around different parts of their bodies in the public wards flanking them. Children, unfortunately, had to view the sick and wounded.

They headed straight for the end of the wing where the intensive care rooms were. Joshua exchanged no words with Maggie the entire time through until they found themselves lost in need of some information. A nurse had just walked by, saving them the hassle as Maggie approached her.

"Hello, my name is Maggie" she diligently introduced herself, with her right hand gesturing by placing it on her chest. "I'm asking after a lady brought in here last night by the name Sarah Abrams."

The nurse wasted no time in acknowledging she knew who the person was.

"How is she, please?" Maggie asked on.

"She's doing okay at the moment," the nurse lady replied. "We've gotten her stabilized, but, are you her family?"

Maggie exchanged a brief look with Joshua before answering; "No, but we're her friends."

The nurse nodded slightly, looking like she had the time to spare with them.

"This is Joshua, a good friend to the patient," she introduced properly, watching Joshua move his hand from his side and towards the nurse.

"Oh, it's nice to meet you," she noted. "Well, I'm glad you're here for her, but she had a severe concussion and broke her neck during the accident last night, and will require some rest and privacy for some time."

"Oh, my God!" Maggie clamped her hand over her mouth upon hearing the sad news. "Can we please see her?"

"We notified her family already, but since you are close to the patient, I guess I could let you see her albeit briefly," the nurse finally conceded. "Would you please help fill some admittance forms that we need to file?"

"Of course, that won't be a problem," Maggie responded, ready to do anything for Sarah.

Joshua had excused himself from them while they were filling out the paperwork. He wasn't asked for his help and had no interest in getting it done. Something about the air felt pressing to him, and he could sense what it was, with the feeling within his guts screaming for him to walk into Sarah's room, which had been pointed out to them by the nurse.

He pushed open the door gently, feeling himself gain unrestricted access into her dimly lit room where he could see clearly, a darkly hooded entity roaming just above Sarah, and swirling around her like a vulture would do its prey. Underneath the cloak, he could see no limbs entirely, while within the darkness provided by the cover, he could make out a pair of glowing red eyes.

He knew what it was immediately, as evident from his acquaintance with it in times past; it was none other than the angel of death, hovering over her, and remaining in wait to strike. It had come to visit her and take her soul when it was ready.

Joshua let the door close behind him, with an extended arm right at the swirling and hovering spirit; "Leave her be this instant!" he yelled in a commanding and unwavering tone. It is not her time.

The angel of death turned to look at him, fleeing instantly from sight upon his command without further delay after making a harmless flight around the room. Joshua approached Sarah, who remained motionless, with tubes stuck into her body from different angles, while her body looked pale and drained of blood from the excessive fluid loss she had suffered during the accident.

He had just gotten to her bed and laid his finger upon the metal bed frame when Sarah woke up with a gasp for air. Her chest inflated, and her eyes widened, with the sudden inflow of air that rushed into her lungs.

She looked around the room slowly, before casting her eyes upon Joshua, who remained standing by the foot of her bed. She stared at him like she had seen a ghost, before speaking in a slight tone indicating she still felt void of her strength.

"I saw you," she recounted her ordeal. "I saw you at the site of my accident," she spoke again.

Joshua smiled without acknowledging or declining what she was saying.

"I was laying on the ground when you spoke to me and assured me I'd be okay," she whispered.

"I wasn't with you, but I guess you could be imagining things," Joshua spoke in a low tone as she did. "If you believe I was there, though, I'm hoping my presence was able to provide you comfort and enough strength to keep strong."

Sarah sighed gently, feeling a strangeness coursing around her body.

"I'm sorry this happened to you, but you'll be fine," he promised her.

Sarah attempted to move her neck but groaned aloud in the process. She could still feel pains shooting round her body in a jet-like manner. Her throat felt parched, and her eyes too heavy to roll around in their sockets. Her body wasn't feeling like it would normally, and she could tell the accident had dealt her more damage than she could come to understand unless the Doctor came to say to her personally.

She was glad Joshua was with her, though, even though she couldn't reach out and touch him by herself. She could see hope brimming in his eyes, and his face provided a warmth she needed then. His presence alone was soothing, but the pain she felt wasn't going away that easily.

"I feel pains Joshua and my head hurts," she informed him, trying to cry, but so parched of bodily liquid and fluid, that no tears came out of her eyes.

Joshua took a few steps to meet with her, gently placing his hand underneath her neck, while the other held her hand, before closing his eyes to say a few prayers.

She could feel an immense power begin to ravage away the pain, with each passing second providing her less pain than the previous. It was strange, but she felt better than she had been for the past few minutes. Joshua gently let go of her body and held his hands behind his back with a few steps away from her.

"Thank you," Sarah appreciated with a weak smile. "Is Maggie with you here in the hospital?"

"Yes, she is, and she wants to see you," he replied to her and heightened her anxiety.

Slowly, Sarah's anxious face turned sour, with thoughts of how horrible she looked and Maggie coming in to see her like that. Joshua could read the signs all over her.

"You need not worry Sarah. Everything will be okay, I promise," Joshua tendered his assurance in certainty. "I'll try to get her to you soon, but you should rest yourself."

Joshua exited the room to meet with Maggie, who thankfully hadn't left where she was filling out the forms with the nurse. She had just gotten through when Joshua got there. Maggie looked at him with questions dancing on her lips.

"She isn't badly hurt, is she? Did she recognize you in any way? Is she going to make it?" in a manner that made Joshua interrupt her before she asked him some more.

"She's doing fine, just badly hurt," he broke the news to her in a soothing way. "She wants to see you. In the meantime, I'll go get myself a cup of coffee," he said to her, before walking away with a bow respectfully.

Maggie rushed away from the nurse, walking as fast as her legs could carry her, while not breaking the hospital's rule about not running in the corridors. She had always known it was wrong from when she was a child, and wouldn't do it, even though she had the burning desire.

Joshua had just taken a right turn into the East wing, when the medics rushed someone past him, wheeling the individual into the operating room in fret and paranoia. He took some minutes to think about the person, before walking toward the elevator, and pressing his thumb on the button for it to open.

The doors widened, and he stepped in, punching the button for the descent to the fourth floor. He felt himself get lighter as the elevator sped down to the fourth floor, where the door opened for him to exit.

He walked right across the hallway, to a room with the door half open, before gently taking a peek inside. Lying on the bed was a child, looking pale and sickly. Her head was bald and loose strands of hair trickle down her face. The girl curiously watched him as he drew closer.

Standing at the foot of her bed, with his arms by his side, he asked her his first question; "What is your name, child?"

"I'm Jenny," the girl slowly replied. "What is your name?" "You can call me Joshua," he replied courteously. "What did the Doctors say is wrong with you?"

She burst into more tears, prompting him to revisit his question in his head.

"My father is late, but my mom just left here some minutes ago," she wept bitterly.

He couldn't take her cries and suffer within him any longer. He prompted his walk toward her, watching her stop crying as he approached, before laying his hand on her shoulder.

"Would you like to pray with me, Jenny?" he asked. "We will pray so you can get better."

She nodded in acceptance, closing her eyes as Joshua did the same.

Fervently he prayed till she fell asleep while holding her. He could see her paleness fade away immediately as he stood up. She looked better than she had been when he walked in earlier, as she tossed gently around in her bed. He excused himself, stepping out of the room without making a sound.

As Joshua walked out of the room, and directly into the one opposite Jenny's, the sight of a boy lying in bed, with a sling around his arm and lifted upward saddened his heart. His right leg was also fitted into the sling, indicating he had a fracture in it as well.

The boy looked scared to move in his state as Joshua approached him.

"Hello, my name is Joshua, what's yours?" he asked.

"My name is Jonathan," the boy struggled to speak.

He sought the reason for his bandaged body, and the boy

narrated how he had broken his arm and leg while riding his skateboard when he visited a skateboard park with his friends. They had enticed him into flying in the air if he could jump into the skateboard pit, and he had done it.

"I shouldn't have listened to them," he murmured. "If I hadn't, I wouldn't be here right now," he lamented.

Joshua got closer to him before sitting by his bedside. "What is your opinion on Jesus, Jonathan?" he asked?

Joshua eyed him curiously. "I know of him, and my mother takes me to church on Sundays."

Joshua nodded in, gladness." You know he can heal you if you have faith in him?"

"Of course, I believe in him," Jonathan attested.

"How about we pray on that so he would heal you quickly?" Joshua asked, placing his hands on the boy's broken limbs.

The prayer was a short one, but Jonathan appreciated it as it came to an end.

"Is there any other thing I can do for you?" Joshua asked his young companion.

"I'm sick of eating the food they serve me here. It's mostly mushy and without taste," Jonathan laid his complaint to Joshua, who chuckled gently. "It makes me want to throw up most times too."

"Let's pray; the nurse brings you something better for lunch," Joshua smiled. "I had better be going. I have quite a lot to do today," he excused himself from the new friend he had made. "You have a good day now."

Joshua had just walked out the door when the nurse brought over Jonathan's meal. She laid down the tray she had in hand on the table, with a stainless steel cover on it and a stainless steel plate housing the contents within. A can of soda stood beside the bowl, while Jonathan wasn't impressed by whatever might be inside.

His frustration was apparent by the look on his face as he stared at the plate without taking his gaze away. He wondered what fresh hell awaited him within the contents of the plate but didn't feel the urge to get it open either. Reluctantly, he stretched his hand to lift the lid off of his plate, to a jaw-dropping sight of what he was staring.

He completely yanked off the cover, hearing the stainless clatter against the table where he tossed it, before admiring the large slices of veggie pizza.

"Oh my God, I can't believe this!" he yelled.

He felt like he was going to cry. He could not believe what he saw. He wondered how it was possible, as he gently opened the bowl to reveal the ice cream within it, which also happened to be his favorite of vanilla.

"This is the best day ever," he muttered aloud. "Thank you, Jesus. Thank you," he said on and on.

Joshua hadn't gone too far, so he heard Jonathan's praise well enough. He approached the hallway with a gladdened heart, walking down the stairway and across another hall, before coming to a halt just by the door of a patient he could see clearly through the transparent glass embedded into the door.

Joshua walked in, watching the man clutch his chest and groaning in pain with an apparent difficulty with something within his chest cavity.

"Are you a doctor? He managed to ask Joshua in a strained tone of voice.

"No, sir, I'm not," Joshua answered him. "My name is Joshua, and I was stretching my feet along the hallways when I heard your cry.

"My name is Marcus," the man spoke.

"It's nice to meet you, Marcus, but why are you here?" Joshua asked. "What ails you, sir?"

"I have a failing heart, Joshua, and I need a new heart valve. "The operation could not be done here." "St. John's Medical Center is the only place," Marcus explained. "I'm waiting for the transport helicopter to arrive."

Joshua could see he was in excruciating pain as he spoke. He groped his chest without letting go, and could barely breathe as he stuttered with every trial to do so without pain. He looked like he was willing to give up hope at any point in time.

"I don't think I will make it," he confessed to Joshua. "I already asked my son to be prepared for my death. I feel very faint."

He gasped for some more air as he spoke. Joshua immediately placed his hand on his chest, beckoning on them to pray together. He could feel the heart failing underneath his touch, while Marcus was merely doing his best to hold on as much as possible. He could feel his hands begin to tremble as well, as they began praying;

"Heavenly Father, please help Marcus in renewing his heart, and relieving him of every pain; he is feeling at the moment. Help him get well so he may live a long, healthy life in the process."

They had just got through praying when Marcus felt a sharp pain in his chest give way before it began easing away ultimately. He felt weaker than before, but better and without pain.

"I feel tired, and I think I'd like to sleep now," he said to Joshua.

The man lay down and fell asleep almost immediately, while Joshua quietly left him and headed back to Sarah's room where Maggie was standing outside the door. She looked relaxed and better than she had been before.

"She's doing okay and recovering faster than they thought," she grinned. "The nurse asked that we let her have some needed rest, and we can come back tomorrow."

"Let's go home," Joshua whispered, smiling from ear to ear.

It was morning in the hospital, and the nurse supervisors had reported different and peculiar activities occurring on their floor to the hospital's director. It was nothing like they had come to see before, and it needed some measure of gathering, which was done by calling together the entire working staff in the hospital.

Dr. Harold Berman, the hospital director, looked from behind his half-moon spectacles around the room where every working medical personnel had assembled as he stood before them. Being a senior man and one of the reputable founders of the hospital for many years, he held a lot of sway in the hospital and gained much respect.

He was a slim man of medium height and with plenty of grey short, balding hair and a well manicured gray beard. He waited for those yet to join them in the conference room before commencing with what he had to say.

"I would like you all to take a moment to halt whatever you're doing and listen to the important message I intend on passing around," he demanded.

The room fell silent, almost immediately into dignity as he had demanded.

"Firstly, I'd like to commend you all on a job well done within the past days, which have been nothing short of extraordinary," he cleared his throat briefly saying. "I'd like to congratulate the Doctors and Nurses for the extra effort put into making sure a good number of grave illnesses got cured."

The Doctors and Nurses were surprised, unable to comprehend what he said. By their standard, they had done the same thing they'd been doing over the years, with no particular change or extra effort applied within the past day or two. The confusion was well set amongst them all, but they kept their thoughts to themselves.

"I'm talking about the extraordinary recoveries reported in the Pediatric and Cardiology wings," Dr. Berman wasn't relenting in his praise.

"I'd love a round of applause for them, please."

The room erupted into applause, before coming to a calm upon the raising of his hand.

"Whatever you all did, keep it up, but let's go have some words with our recovered patients," he said, leading the way out of the conference room.

Those around could barely understand anything about what he was saying, except for the medical personnel working on the floors where the events had come to occur. They followed behind like sheep would do with their shepherd. The first room they visited was the little girl previously diagnosed with cancer. With her head shaved for the chemotherapy session.

Her mother was sitting in the room, just by her daughter with a glad look all over her, and a mix of curiosity as she watched her daughter in a different light from when she had seen her for the past week. She looked full of life, and unlike the sick girl, she had been for a while. The confusion only grew as the doctors walked in to inquire.

"What is going on with my daughter?" she turned to the first nurse to walk in.

She was the lead nurse in the cancer unit as well as the pediatric unit of the hospital and someone they had gotten to know well enough. She was a tall, middle-aged woman, white, with hazel high-lighted brown hair worn in a bun, and pale green eyes, wearing a white uniform. The nurse was always beautiful to them and never wore a frown even when she was tired and overworked.

"You have nothing to worry about ma'am," she said to Jenny's mother. "Your daughter has been healed of her cancer, with no traces lurking in her system."

Jenny's mother looked to her daughter, who was playing with her doll, and then back at the nurse. She couldn't fathom what she was told.

"I want to believe in it nurse, trust me, and with all my heart, but how is that possible?" she asked, trying not to doubt what the woman was telling her.

"We ran all the tests, trust me, she's clean and free of cancer," she assured Jenny's mother who had just erupted into tears of joy.

She felt overjoyed like never before as she showed her appreciation by hugging the nurse gladly. The doctors standing around watched with raised eyebrows, and the inability to fathom what was going on. The doctors tried conceiving the best possible explanations in their heads, with curiosity looming in their hearts.

Most of them concluded that her body had merely healed itself, which was something possible in some cases. They couldn't see past it is the natural healing of the body cells to survive and sustain life. It was the only viable medical explanation they could concede.

Dr. Berman led them out of the room to the next occurrence, which was to visit the young man who had broken his arm and leg in an accident. They met him standing and getting dressed. He looked ready to leave the hospital, having gotten tired of their meals and the air in Commander.

"Nurse, I believe I can go now, can't I?" the young boy said.

"Of course sweetie, you can," she acknowledged his question.

"There's no trace of any broken bone in your body."

The doctors knew of his case, the day he was rushed into the hospital on an emergency when the incident occurred. It took some doing by their best team to get the bones set into place, before helping him into a bandage. The fact he was standing was something unnatural and impossible. He shouldn't be able to move any of the broken parts, let alone be moving around.

"How can this be?" a doctor asked. "I saw the x-ray myself and helped in his dressing, so this shouldn't be possible in any way."

"I can't say anything other than the x-ray machine could be faulty and gave an image of someone else's fracture," she replied.

Dr. Berman walked closer to the boy. He took a long look at the boy, examining him from head to toe. He needed to see things for himself before saying anything.

"Aren't you in pain?" he asked the young man who felt relieved to be out of his cast.

"Pain? I haven't felt that since yesterday," he responded. "I can dance, watch me," he added, tapping his feet aggressively against the floor. "Look, I can dance again!" he yelled atop his voice in joy. "I'm ready to go home.

"I'm sure you are... ," Dr. Berman was speaking when a nurse from the cardiac unit interrupted him. The nurse was a short, curvy young black woman wearing light blue scrubs. She had black curly hair and wore thin wire-rim glasses.

"Sir, you need to have a look at the next patient," she informed him impatiently like she needed them all to see.

The entire staff proceeded to the Cardiology section. The man with the heart problem was down the hall with his son, rearing to leave. He chimed with happiness, hugging, and shaking hands with his son. He was cheering with joy as they approached him.

"I feel wonderful like I have a new heart valve," he said. "Look, I can do pushups and jumping jacks like during the time I was in the Army."

He began to flap both of his arms and jumped up and down erratically. He dropped to the floor and did his pushups as he used to without any form of constraint from his heart. The doctors looked at him with curiosity and could not explain what happened the evening before.

"It's impossible for someone with such a heart condition to be doing any of this," a young doctor spoke. "Are we certain it wasn't just heartburn. Did we misdiagnosed him?"

" No, we diagnosed him correctly," the nurse corrected the doctor.

They were all left in a state of mental limbo, unable to decipher how it had come to be. Their efforts to assemble the occurrences into one solid reasoning were impossible, and they failed at every turn. Dr. Berman had heard enough to call their attention and focus on himself.

He needed to address them.

"Dear colleagues, I believe what we have witnessed here today is nothing short of miracles, and we will or might never come to understand how it came to be," he informed them. "I believe it was some form of blessing from above, and I've never seen anything like it in all my life and years in the profession."

Those around nodded in acknowledgment and believed that was what had happened.

"I'd advise that we keep this to ourselves discreetly, to avoid any unneeded attention and investigation this would surely bring us should it get out, and the press gets wind of this," he warned them. "What happened here was nothing but a miracle and one we will hold with us to our graves." They all nodded in compliance.

CHAPTER 5

ack to *Maggie's Bed and Breakfast*
Joshua and Maggie arrived at her establishment and
stood on the porch briefly to think things through. She
looked less burdened than she had been before they visited the
hospital and more relaxed at the moment.

"Do you have some wood and tools?" Joshua asked her with his
gaze staring into the distance.

She turned to him; "My late husband may have a few in work
shed at the back of the house, just over the yonder," she responded.
"You're welcome to make use of it." "Thank you, I'll do just that," he
assured her.

Joshua walked around the back of the house. The grass was
slightly tall, and there was a small pebble trail leading to the wooden
shed. The woodshed had a metal roof, and the windows were dirty,
and it made seeing through them very much impossible.

Right in front of the door was a screen door, which he opened
gently, before going into the entrance. He walked in, approaching a

large wooden table. On the table, there were some tools with which he could work. They ranged from saws to hammers and other necessary equipment a carpenter would need.

He admired the tools briefly, noting how wonderful a collection they were.

He bent over to help himself to some of the needed tools with which he was going to use, laying them aside gently. He then found some pieces of solid oak lying on the floor across from him, just a short distance from the table. He was sure the wood would make a sturdy chair, so he helped himself to a few pieces and laid them on the table.

Next, to the table, there was a rusty old foot-powered lathe with parts that were rusted and frozen. Joshua rubbed his hands on the metal parts vigorously, including the flywheel and spindle, and the rust disappeared almost immediately after a few tries.

He immediately began to work on Maggie's rocking chair. He started by cutting the pieces of wood into desired shapes and sizes, before cutting out the seat, the armrest, and the parts to make the legs. He took a bit for the curved header and grabbed a chisel and hammers and began to carve a symbol on the header. It was a tree with rays protruding from the tree.

He then carved two angels on each side similar to the Ark of the Covenant and made a hole on the armrest for Maggie to place her glass of tea. He sanded the entire rocking chair and burnished it with Tung oil he found in the shed and allowed it dry. He permitted it enough time to dry, before moving close to admire his handwork carefully.

He was confident it was perfect, before he picked up the rocking chair, and went ahead to place it on Maggie's porch. Afterward, he went in search for Maggie, to inform her of her new rocking chair, with the feeling she was going to love it upon seeing it. He went inside the house and walked into the living room area but could not find her.

He could see only the guests chattering away in her absence. Joshua interrupted one of the guests reading a book. "Excuse me, but do you know where Maggie is?"

He pointed towards the kitchen; "She's in the kitchen, I believe."

Joshua ran into the kitchen, where he saw Maggie making a cake.

"Maggie, I just finished your rocking chair, come outside and check it out," he informed her with his breath challenging to come by.

All excitedly, she wiped her hands on her apron before removing it and placing it on the table. Joshua stole a peek at the cake she was making, feeling enticed by the sweet vanilla icing smeared upon it. He extended his finger towards it, wiping off a little bit to lick.

"This tastes good," he said to her, reaching for another lick when she slapped his hand off of the icing.

"The cake is for our dessert, after dinner," she warned him, pulling him by his shirt out of the kitchen to save the cake from untimely death and burial in his stomach. "You may have as much as you want later."

She followed Joshua outside to the porch, anxiously to see the rocking chair. As she got closer and saw the delicate and intricate work, he has done she became ecstatic.

"Oh My God!" she said. "I've never seen anything like this, especially the carving on the headrest. It so beautiful."

She rubbed her hand over the carving, trailing it with her finger to have a feel of what he had inscribed into the piece of wood. It felt, unlike anything she had seen before, with its uniqueness something she appreciated immediately.

"Sit and give it a swing will you," Joshua asked of her. Maggie slowly sat down, having no understanding of just how comfortable it was going to be until she finally let herself ease into it, and made contact with the seat. Maggie relieved her weight with the help of her hands, using the armrest provided, feeling her tiredness ease off without warning. She adjusted in it, feeling how comfortable it was as she stole a gaze at Joshua, before looking back at the chair.

"This feels so comfortable it might just be the best chair I've ever sat down in as gushed in with so much excitement.

Slowly, she rocked the chair forward and backward in an oscillatory motion with a wild smile on her face. She had just noticed the cup holder and found it helpful as well as conveniently set in place without having to disturb her armrest when she places her hand on them.

"I love the cup holder you put into it as well," she said in gratitude. "It's beautiful."

'I'm glad you like it,' he replied, feeling the job was well done and appreciated.

Maggie intended using the holders built into the chair for her cup and magazines while enjoying some fresh air outside.

"I'm going to spend a lot of time on this chair and do my bible readings here," she explained to him.

"I even made a book holder on the side for you where you can keep your bible," he showed to her.

"Well, will you look at that, you thought of everything," Maggie grinned. I will take you to see the Pastor tomorrow. "I spoke with him, and he wants to talk to you about building those new pews."

"I'm looking forward to that," he said.

~

The following morning Maggie took Joshua to the Pastor. They drove to the Church in her truck. As they arrived at the Church, they heard the choir practicing their songs aloud in musical tones. Maggie sang along to the ones she knew before turning to Joshua.

"Do you sing Joshua?" she asked, seeing he had been expecting the question with his eyes gleaming back at her.

"No, I don't," Joshua replied to her. "I've never been much of the kind to sing, as I guess my father never gave me the gift to."

She funnily looked at him for the words in the latter end of his sentence but brushed it away.

"I once sang when I was younger," said Maggie. As I got older, my voice got a bit rougher and derailed. She further commented just as the Pastor came closer to them.

He walked to them diligently, with each stride taking just about a normal gait till he got to them. He had a smile on his face and shook their hands before speaking.

"Hello, I am Pastor Ed Brown, I heard so much about you and Maggie told me you're the best furniture maker she's ever seen," he introduced himself with a little smear of flattery towards Joshua.

Joshua couldn't help himself from not blushing, trying hard as he could to fail though.

"I always give my best in everything I do," he spoke.

"If that be the case, I need ten new pews, and I need them within one month before the Thanksgiving holidays." "You don't mind doing them for me that soon, I hope?" Pastor Ed asked.

"I'll work tirelessly to get them ready before then," he assured Pastor Ed.

"That would be great Joshua, and you can make them out of

solid oak, or maple, while I'd like them to be at least 10 Ft. long and sturdy enough to hold at least five people," he described in full his specifications. "I'll have my maintenance men pick them up and pay for them when they are completed."

Joshua showed his gratitude, by smiling and expelling it through words; "I appreciate the opportunity you're giving to me," he said. "I'll build you the best pews you've ever seen."

Maggie interjected with her look.

"I believe we don't have enough wood in the storage shed to make the pews," she pointed out. "We need to go get some more at the Lumberyard. I can drive you there."

Looking rather sadly, Joshua told Maggie; "I don't have any money to buy wood."

"Don't worry, it'll be my piece of contribution," she assured him, to lay his worry to rest.

"Maggie, I cannot accept you are paying for them. You have already done enough for me by giving me a roof over my head, and food to eat," he declined respectfully.

"Don't be like that," she warned him. "I simply need to help the church get those pews."

"Well, in that case, I'll let you buy the wood, but I would request that I place a plaque on the pews with your name, so people know that you contributed," Joshua suggested.

Maggie smiled at how thoughtful he was. "If the Pastor deems it good enough, then I have no worries with it."

~

They headed back out to the car, getting into it, while Maggie drove Joshua to the lumber yard which was a few miles from the Church.

They arrived at Stockman's Lumberyard where they could hear the saws roaring and cutting through the wood as they stepped out of the car.

Joshua took his time to examine the site, looking fascinated by what he saw. At a distance, he saw a large spinning circular saw blade enter the bottom of a wooden log. The saw began to cut the log, and he could hear the high pitch ringing of the blade split the log into boards. Wood chips started to fly in all directions. The gears of the conveyor belt started whirring as the board fell onto the conveyor belt. The belt moved the board upward toward a large bin where he saw the wood drop with a loud thump. "Interesting," Joshua commented.

"They're one of the largest lumber manufacturers in these parts," Maggie said to him.

They walked side by side towards the building, entering it before walking up to the counter where a tall man with a beard and bald head stood watching them come right in.

"Hello, I'm Joe, how may I be of service to you?" he asked. "Hello, I'm Joshua, we need some church pews, and we'd like to make them out of Oak or Maple" he explained to the man who stared at him the entire time while listening.

"Okay, how much are you going to need?" Joe asked.

"Well, we need to make ten pews, and each has to be approximately 10ft," Joshua exchanged a glance with Maggie saying. He wanted to be sure he wasn't missing or forgetting anything.

"Our price for the Maple is less than the Oak," Joe explained. "The Oak is way more expensive, but the Maple does an excellent job for you as well."

There was no debating it; Maggie opted for the Maple with a chuckle. They watched Joe handle himself with his calculator, multiplying figures on it to ascertain the price of wood they intended to get.

"You're going to need more wood for the head and rails if I'm correct," he spoke without looking at them. "This would be your cost after everything I believe," he finally got through, handing them the calculator.

Maggie took one good look at the charge he was tendering and gave the calculator back to him. She was not impressed.

"Can you do any better please? This is for a church, you know?" she reminded him.

Joe took a deep breath and let it all back out. He punched the numbers again on the calculator and then showed it to Maggie.

"This is the best I can do sorry," he said to her.

"I don't think we are quite there yet," Maggie declined to look at him in the opposite direction.

Joe yelled at her, "Lady; I can't give the wood away, you know?" Joe declined to ease the price lower any further.

"The Lord will bless your business tremendously if you give us a better price," she prayed for him, hoping it would enable him towards helping them.

Joe shook his head worryingly, feeling a trickle of sweat down his back. He had met ladies like Maggie and knew they don't budge until they got what they wanted. Joshua just said nothing, leaving them both to transact since it wasn't his money they were playing with, and Maggie seemed to be a better bargainer than he would.

Joe punched the buttons on the calculator harder and in frustration again, before showing it to her as the final price he could go low on. He looked sweaty now, and uncomfortable, but he managed to hide his discomfort well enough.

"I'd be good to take this, I believe," she said satisfied.

They both sighed in relief before Maggie demanded to know about the delivery bill, which wasn't added to the original invoice, and was well needed since Joshua couldn't come to pick them up himself.

"That would be $75," he informed her with a grin, knowing he wasn't and couldn't reduce the price even if he wanted to.

"How about you throw that into the price for a hot apple pie?" she teased, watching the man's eyes widen.

"Trust me, it's a wonderful offer because she makes a mean apple pie," Joshua finally spoke, backing Maggie in her pursuit of an economical price.

"Put a ball of Vanilla ice cream on it, and you'd think you went to heaven," she enticed him some more into taking her offer, which in actuality wasn't a bad one.

Joe had begun to salivate with his eyes sternly, looking at her as she spoke. He smacked his lips gently at the thought of the apple pie, before giving a soft sight.

"Okay, I'll take the pie, but not a piece of it, but the entire pie," he warned.

"You got yourself a deal, Joe," Maggie congratulated him. "My name is Maggie, by the way."

"Thank you, Maggie," he appreciated.

"I will have it ready in a box when you deliver the wood. Here is my business card," she handed him the sheet with her contact details on it. "I want you to deliver the wood to this address."

Joe took his time to breeze through the address with his eyes before returning it to his drawer.

"When can you deliver it?" she asked?

"First thing in the morning," said Joe.

"That would be wonderful, thank you," Maggie chimed, taking out her purse to pay the bill as intended.

They bid their goodbyes to Joe, who gladly did the same while smiling, upon recalling his encounter with Maggie.

"You sure know how to drive a hard bargain," Joshua teased her. "I should take you to the common market with me when I have some money to do my intended shopping," he joked.

Maggie laughed out loud. She took it as a compliment, and he had intended it as such.

"Being a single woman with no one to help you, and having to make ends meet on your own, brings that side out of you," she chuckled.

As Joshua got back to the car, he nodded tenderly. "You're a resourceful woman Maggie," he commented her as she drove out.

"Thank you, dear," she merely whispered, and they drove off.

～

As promised and paid for, on the expected morning, the truck from Stockman's lumber yard came. The delivery man walked to the door and knocked on it briefly. As she opened the door, the creaking sound of the door reminded her to ask Joshua if he could lubricate the hinges.

"I have a delivery for Ms. Maggie," the tall and muscular man with dark hair and brown eyes wearing a blue button-down shirt with the Stockman's logo on it.

"That would be me, thank you," she smiled, casting a look over their shoulders at the delivery.

"Where would you like to have the lumber dropped?" he asked.

Maggie led them to the back of the storage, where the man

agreed to drop the lumber he brought in. The man walked up to the forklift that was connected to his flatbed truck and dropped it down to the ground. He turned the key and started up the forklift, and a puff of white smoke blew out of the muffler. He moved the forklift close to the flatbed truck and carefully pulled the lift lever. He then lifted the fork onto the wooden pallet where the wood laid. Maggie curiously watched him lifting the pallet and dropping the wood in front of the shed. Once he had finished, he asked Maggie to sign the delivery receipt, which she signed.

The man had just turned his back and was about to leave when she called for him to halt. He turned to her with querying looks.

"Is anything wrong, ma'am?" he asked.

"No, I need for you to give something to Joe for me," she informed him.

Maggie ran into the kitchen to pick up the pie from the stove top and place it in a white box. The pieces of the pie were already divided, before giving the box to the delivery guy. She informed him to give it to Joe, before heading back inside to the breakfast area, where Joshua was drinking some orange juice. Maggie told Joshua of the delivery, and he greeted the news with some level of excitement.

"I'll start working on the pews right away," he said.

The delivery man drove off while Maggie watched him leave right through the front road. The delivery man had one more load of wood to deliver and drove to his next stop. He looked down on the passenger seat where he had placed the box with the pie. It sure smells good, he said. Let me see what's inside. His eyes widened, and he began to savor the aroma of fresh baked apples and cinnamon as his mouth watered. He slowly opened the box and saw the pie. Boy, that looks good he said. He picked up one slice. It was a large one. He bit into it. "Um," he said reflectively. "Um-um!" His eyes widened, and he clutched his throat. Juice from the apple pie started to drip down his shirt. He grabbed a small towel he had laying next to him and wiped the stain off his shirt. He then grabbed his metal Yeti Tumbler, which was filled with coffee and took a swig of coffee to wash down the apple pie. "Man that was good," he said. "I think I will have another slice." After he dropped the last load of wood, he proceeded on to Stockman's Lumber yard to drop off the flatbed truck. He walked inside the store and saw Joe standing behind the counter.

"Did you deliver the wood to Maggie's B&B," asked Joe?

"I sure did," said the delivery man. "Oh, by the way, she gave me this box for you." Great, I am glad she kept her word. The delivery man walked towards the time clock hanging on the wall and grabbed his punch card. He placed the punch card inside the slot, and a loud click sounded. He took the punch card out and placed it on the holder amongst the other cards. "Good night," said the delivery man. "You have a great weekend." Joe began to stare at the box and said to himself. "I will try a piece of her pie now." He placed both hands on the box and slowly began to open it. "No, I better not. I will ruin my dinner, and my wife will kill me. I will take it home and share it with my wife." He looked at the box again. He could not resist the temptation to get a bit of that delicious apple pie Joshua told him. "Oh, what the hell one small piece will not hurt," he said. He grabbed both ends of the box with his hands and began to open it slowly. To his amazement, all he saw were slithers of crust and crumbs. "Well, I will be dam," Joe said. "I am going to give my driver a piece of pie right in his face when he comes back to work."

Joshua proceeded to the woodshed to begin work by picking up the wood pieces one after the other and laying them to rest on the table to cut them. He intended to work tirelessly, which he did until nightfall when they had gotten completed.

He had just gotten through and began burnishing when he heard the unmistakable sound of Sarah's car driving up to the house. Maggie ran as fast as her legs could carry her, to go and meet with her.

"I'm so happy you're doing okay," Maggie said gladly, noticing that Sarah was wearing a neck brace around her neck.

"The Doctor said I was lucky," Sarah giggled.

"I don't believe in such luck, honey, but I believe the Lord was there with you all the way."

"I still have to return to the hospital for some additional tests," Sarah enlightened her friend. "I have a few bruises, but the pain is all gone."

They shared a warm hug after she had talked about being okay before Maggie peeled herself away from the woman.

"I took Joshua to the Pastor, and he gave him the contract to make the church's pews," Maggie broke the good news to Sarah.

Sarah smiled as hard as she could, sharing in the happiness that Joshua had gotten the job. "I'm happy to hear that."

Joshua walked over to them to share his news as well.

"I'm almost finished with them, would you care to look at them?" he said before greeting Sarah warmly.

Sarah accepted his invitation with gladness, as he led the ladies to the work shed where the ten pews were. They all looked so beautiful, very well polished and burnished without a fault. The pews also had pockets in the back.

"I made the pockets so you can place your bibles there and also a smaller pocket to place the new member forms and also to place pens or pencils," he explained.

Maggie and Sarah were delighted with Joshua's work.

"I think the Pastor is going to be impressed with your work," Sarah acknowledged.

"Is the Pastor going to need cushions and fabric on the seat?" Joshua asked to know.

"Not really," said Maggie. "I don't think the Pastor will want to go through the expense." "Sarah, you need to see the rocking chair Joshua built for me."

She pulled her friend along cautiously to show it to her like a prized possession as they walked up to the porch together. Sarah took a pretty good look at the chair, examining every part of it before giving her comment, while Joshua waited for it to come. If there was one thing he had come to know, it was that Sarah was a vocal lady in her way.

"Oh my God this is a beautiful rocking chair," she shrieked. "Joshua, can you make me one too?"

Joshua smiled, "Of course I can." "There should be enough wood in the shed for one more, and I can start on it right away."

Maggie butted in; "Perhaps later, but not now after the tireless work you've been doing all day, and you look tired."

CHAPTER 6

hanksgiving Services

On Thanksgiving Day, the entire parking lot was filled with cars, leaving others to find a place to park their vehicles elsewhere. All of the pews were full of Church Attendees, but Sarah, Maggie, and Joshua had arrived early. They came first to get a seat close to the stage so they could listen to the Pastor welcome everyone and wish everyone a Happy Thanksgiving.

He gave thanks for the day and said a prayer.

"I would like you all to take note of the beautiful pews you're sitting. A new member of ours by the name Joshua made them " Pastor Ed informed the Church in a brief announcement.

Everyone applauded Joshua's work, showing how much they loved the pews he had made.

Joshua smiled and bowed down to demonstrate his appreciation in the process of their applause.

"How about Joshua coming up to lead the congregation by

reading some scriptures in the bible for us?" Pastor Ed said, putting Joshua on the spot.

Joshua accepted his offer and began to march up to the stage. The Pastor shook his hand and walked him to the podium, where he helped place the lapel microphone on him. Joshua wasn't looking nervous or shaky in any way as he cleared his throat to speak.

"Today we are going to learn about Thessalonians," said Pastor Ed, as he showed Joshua the specific spot in the bible scripture.

Joshua smirked, raising his shoulders, before raising the bible and closing it respectfully. Pastor Ed couldn't help but cast him a worrisome look as well as a raised eyebrow. Joshua had just begun speaking into the microphone when a shrieking and deafening noise reached their ears. It was interference causing the microphone to misbehave.

"Help him adjust the microphone," Pastor Ed asked of his assistant who obeyed immediately.

Joshua readjusted himself, gaining a better countenance; before he began to read Thessalonian's word for word without looking at the bible. He recounted the precise words by heart like they were right there scribbled in the air for him to read, forcing the Pastor to gaze into his bible to be sure the man was reading out the correct scripture.

He finally raised his head to look around the church, and behold; every single person therein was amazingly looking at him. They seemed in awe that he could do all that without looking at the bible.

"He must have had an eidetic memory," a woman told her neighbor, who merely nodded.

Joshua heard her but continued his preaching in alluring words that made them all listen to him attentively. He made a habit of interpreting every scripture he gave with examples to help them understand better. He talked about corruption and how God destroyed Sodom and Gomorrah.

"We're living together in a world that is becoming more like Sodom and Gomorrah, and God is upset," he preached. "We have to make an effort to prevent this from happening and to bring it to the attention of people throughout the world to stop this corruption."

Some of the people began to laugh out loud. He continued without listening to their laughter.

"There are lots of people who have moved away from God," he said to them. "Although you haven't seen or heard from him, he knows what everyone you does and he records all of your actions." He warmed further.

Some sections of the church fell silent as he spoke on.

"He writes all of your actions in his book, and he keeps a record on each and everyone one of you," he gestured with every part of his body to show them he meant every word. "He wonders if you will continue to defile his commandments and keep on with your bad in this world. Each year he reviews your book, and he will decide if you are worthy of entering into his kingdom upon your death."

The entire congregation fell silent still, making no sound. "We must have hope and pray that he forgives the ones that.

sin," Joshua continued. "He allowed his son to die on the cross for our sins, yet they forget and continue to sin."

Everyone agreed with him by nodding, except for one person who stood up. He was a heavy-set man with blond hair, gray eyes and wore a baseball cap, blue cotton coveralls, and a jacket. He spoke with a southern accent:

"That is nothing but a bunch of crap, and I blatantly disagree with you," he voiced. "God has abandoned us, and as far as I know and am concerned, he is nowhere to be found and could be dead just like we're all going to die."

The entire church gasped at what the man said, while Joshua just stared at him. He knew his kind and exactly what was going through the man's head, but made no intent to speak harshly toward him. The Pastor walked over to take over the podium, easing Joshua out of the spot.

"Let's pray to God for and about everything Joshua had just told us," he asked of those in the church.

Joshua bowed his head like everyone did, praying in line with everything he had just preached.

> *Father, please help us deviate from the path of corruption. We have faith in you and the words that you and your disciples have written and engraved into our hearts and mind. Be able to help us teach that to our children so that our world will not become corrupted and help us change the mind of those that want to follow Satan's path. Help us bring the holy spirit into everyone's body and change the course of history to better humankind. In our father's name, I pray, Amen."*

"Thank you, Joshua, you may be seated," Pastor Ed beckoned him before Joshua went back to his seat as asked. "Today, I want to discuss my favorite scripture in Revelations. Please turn to Chapter 2:17."

Everyone opened up their bibles to the mentioned verse and began reading through.

"To he or she who has ears, let them listen carefully to what this

verse has to say," Pastor Ed warned. "This is what the spirit says to the church... "
"

    I will give the victor some of the hidden manna. I will also give him a white stone, and on that stone, a new name is inscribed that no one knows except the one who receives it."

"As God gave those believers a new name, so shall he do for you," he prophesied into their lives. "I will give everyone here today a natural white stone, quarried near Bethlehem and Hebron," he told them. "It is hand cut and tumbled, and when you receive this stone, I want you to take the pencil that they will give you and write what you to want the Lord to bless you with," he instructed.

He instructed them on what to do next, which was to write what they sought God for as regards any miracle or favor they needed granted into their lives, before turning the stone to its other side and writing a new biblical name of their choice on it as well. He asked for the name to be a biblical one that they intended for people to call them with hence.

"I want you all to be known by that name and to use the name throughout the year. It could also serve as a nickname," he said.

Some in the crowd shouted "Buba" while a section of the Congregation began to laugh.

"That is too common," said the Pastor. "Pick something original."

The Pastor's helpers picked up the basket of stones and began to pass them around. Everyone in the Congregation passed the basket while picking up a stone. Each person picked up a stone and pencil, including Sarah and Joshua. The natural stone was rectangular and measured approximately 2 inches by 1 inch. It was hand cut and tumbled. It was milky white, rough, and chalky. Sarah took the pencil and wrote down the word "Grace."

Sarah then looked at Joshua, who had just written down "Humiliation."

She was struck with wonder as she whispered the word without realizing she had.

"What's that about?" she asked him, just about the time Pastor Ed was speaking again?

"Now, I implore you all to keep the blessing to yourself; however, you can share the name with your friends and family," he said. "Now I want everyone to turn the stone around and write your new name on the other side."

Sarah turned over the stone, and to her amazement, there was a name already written on her stone. It was the name "Abraham."

She gasped in disbelief, thinking it was some joke; "Oh my God." She looked around slowly before speaking; "My last name is Abrams and not Abraham, who wrote this."

"Maybe the Lord wants you to be called Abraham in honor of your great, great grandfather," said Joshua.

"How could I have gotten a stone with the name written on it? Maybe someone is pulling a joke on me. Every stone must have my new last name on it already," she doubted, reaching over to see Joshua's, which had nothing but a blank face on it.

"That's pretty much weird," she noted, feeling uncomfortable by what she was staring.

Sarah returned the stone to Joshua, and he looked down at the word "Humiliation" again that he had penned down earlier. He stared at the stone and went into a trance. He envisioned the day he washed his disciples' feet during his last supper. For him, it was not a humiliation but an act of humbleness. His disciples had said on that day; "Rabbi it is we who should wash your feet, not you."

Sarah interrupted Joshua's thinking by placing the tithe plate on his lap. Joshua stared at the word once more, before turning the stone over to the other side, which now had the name "Yeshua," written on it. He hadn't written it obviously, but it cranked a smile across his face as he placed the stone on the plate.

Before dismissing the Congregation, the Pastor announced the need for volunteers at the food bank to feed the poor with their Thanksgiving meals, and whoever was free during lunch was more than welcome to give a helping hand.

Sarah turned to Joshua and said; "Would you care to volunteer?"

"Of course," Joshua replied with a look wondering why she would even doubt him. "I'd be honored to feed the hungry."

Sarah turned to Maggie to ask the same question, hoping her friend would be around to share the time with her and Joshua.

"Maggie, how about you?" she smiled.

"I would have loved to, but you know I have to go back home and finish cooking our Thanksgiving meal, which you're all invited to tonight," she explained. "I'm cooking a huge turkey with all the trimmings and all the sides, and for dessert, some pumpkin, and pecan pie."

"That sounds delicious, and I'm sure Sarah and I wouldn't miss it for anything in the world," Joshua assured her.

Sarah turned her head to Joshua carefully before seconding his every word. "Maggie's cooking is out of this world, and I wouldn't miss it."

"I believe it is," Joshua chimed.

CHAPTER 7

⚜

Feeding the poor

  The food bank was temporarily at the Veterans Hall. The patrons waited patiently to be served and lined out the door.

Joshua and Sarah met with John, who ran the Food Bank.

"We have to get the food out and place it on the warming trays, and we need to keep these trays warm all of the time at the correct temperature otherwise the food inspector will shut us down when they make their inspection," John informed them. "They should make two rounds today."

Joshua and Sarah immediately went to work together by placing the food on the pans. They lighted the heat canisters and set the containers above them. Sliced turkey, dressing, sweet potatoes, mash potatoes, green beans, hot rolls, cranberry sauce and pumpkin pie for dessert filled the trays. The food lines were already getting set, and John went up to the door to unlock it. He opens the door and stuck his head outside to see the amazingly long line.

"There sure are lots of people out here," he cried out to Sarah from where he stood. "Folks, the food is ready, and you can come in now," He ushered them along as best as he could. "We have plenty of food for everyone, so no cutting in line, everyone will be served."

The people formed one line, and they were all well mannered. Sarah and Joshua, among the other three workers, began filling the trays with food while the people took their turns to get served. Joshua got a quick hang of it, while Sarah seemed like a pro who had been doing it for a very long time.

"Would you care for one or two rolls?" she asked a man standing before her waiting to get his food.

Some opted for two, while others took just one, depending on how well their belly could hold their food. Everyone receiving a food tray thanked Sarah, Joshua, and the team as they got served, and it was a lovely experience for them all. Sarah instructed Joshua to fill the tea canister and put ice in the cups and made sure everyone had plenty of food and drink.

"Do we have enough cups?" She asked him as he set about carrying out her order.

Joshua just smiled back at her to say, "Yes, we have plenty to go around," before returning to his spot to continue serving.

The line kept coming, and all of sudden John began looking worried. He looked over at Sarah with his worried expression to inform her and the team that they were running out of food.

"I don't know what we can do, but we might have to close down," he informed the team in a disheartening voice. "The food we have just won't be enough for everyone."

"That won't be good," Sarah noted, while they took a brief moment to mull things through.

"I have to let them know," John said painfully. He turned to the people waiting for food, informing them that they might have to close due to a shortage of food, with moans and groans meeting his announcement.

He felt terrible, but there was nothing he could do about it. "I did not expect so many people this year, and we have very little turkey left," he told his team.

"Perhaps we can start giving smaller portions," Sarah suggested, in a bid to make sure everyone got food.

"No, I don't think that is going to work out," John shook his head. "People will complain and be hungry, which we can't risk, so we'll have to disappoint a few and close when we can."

Joshua had kept silent while they spoke, before interjecting; "Wait here a minute," he asked of them.

They watched him take the empty pan of turkey with a small piece left in the tray as well as an empty container of rolls before running into the back of the room with it and out of their sight. There, alone and unseen, he began to pray as best as he could, before opening his eyes to the view of more sliced turkey and rolls which started to stack on the pan one by one until the pans were full to the brim.

Joshua multiplied the portion the same way he did in ancient times when there was not enough fish and bread for his disciples and believers. He ran out from the back to call Sarah and John to help him out with carrying the food.

"Sarah, can you give me a hand in here please?" he asked politely, while she ran into the back of the room to assist him. "Help me pick up those pans," he said to them.

John gasped in shock, feeling unsure of what he was looking at until he went to handle it with his hands. He looked back at Joshua, who didn't seem fazed or perplexed by the strange occurrence in any way.

"Where did you get all this from?" he was forced to ask. "I saw nothing here when I came to check earlier."

With his hands behind his back, and a straight face, Joshua replied; "There could be the possibility you had overlooked them."

John looked at the food again and shook his head in disagreement with Joshua.

"No, I'm sure I saw nothing more here when I came," he reiterated.

Sarah smiled at Joshua while John began to doubt his eyes. "I guess I'm going to have to get my eyes examined," the man said. "I just can't believe it."

They conveyed the food items back to the service area, where the line refused to dwindle, but they were more than up to the task, providing for everyone who had come to get fed. The lines kept going, but there was enough food to feed everyone.

When the last person left, they closed the doors, and they began to clean the trays. Joshua took the trash out to the back and dumped the bags of waste in the dumpster. He then went back inside to continue helping others. He had just arrived while Sarah was speaking to the rest of the team.

"It was a lot of work, but I must confess to enjoying the fact we were able to feed those in need and who couldn't afford a Thanksgiving meal," she commended them all and herself.

"Well-done Job guys," John congratulated them as well. "I hope to meet you all here next year, and I must confess I couldn't have done it without you guys."

"Happy Thanksgiving guys," Joshua acknowledged everyone before he and Sarah took their leave.

They headed off to the car, where Sarah had begun muttering about the food they had thought was finished.

"I can't believe John overlooked that much food earlier," she cracked herself up with laughter. "If there was nothing, how did all that food appear?"

Joshua looked at Sarah sternly. "I would imagine it was the work of the Father who provides when there is a necessity. He gave manna to the Jews when they were in the wilderness, and he gives abundance to those that believe in him. He made the water into wine. All you have to do is pray for help, and you shall receive."

Sarah stared hard into Joshua's eyes, doubting him all the way. She leaned closer to him, wondering if he had somehow protected enough of the food items knowing they might run out early enough, before bringing them out again. She had gotten close to the point her lips were well able to connect with his, but he held her back by her hand.

He gently kissed her hand, showing affection towards her, but enough to tell he had no intent on getting into a relationship or any form of intimacy with her. She shyly withdrew her hand, getting into the car as the sun began to set. They drove back to Maggie's place, arriving at dusk.

~

They walked up to the wooden stairs as Sarah looked over at the rocking chair Joshua had made.

"I just may ask Maggie if I can buy the rocking chair from her and take it home tonight," she joked, causing them both to erupt into laughter as they walked through the door to the sight of a table already set by Maggie.

She had a charming handmade tablecloth and her finest china set on the table in wait for them. Maggie set the dinnerware for six people, including Sarah, Joshua, herself, and some of her guests staying at her house whom she had personally invited.

Usually, she would have served breakfast alone, but being a special day, and nowhere for her guests to go for Thanksgiving, she had decided to invite them over. They all sat down gingerly while Maggie brought out the turkey. It was a gigantic roasted whole turkey stuffed with cornbread dressing and surrounded by a bed of lettuce on a large platter adorned with cherry tomatoes around it.

Joshua exchanged a quick look with Sarah, who seemed to be disappointed about the turkey since she was a vegetarian. However, Maggie returned to the kitchen and came back out with sweet rolls, sides of sweet potatoes, cranberry sauce, mashed potatoes, green bean casserole, dressing, gravy, pumpkin pie and, pecan pie. Sarah's eyes widened once she saw the sides and began to show a sign of relief. Joshua sat at the head of the table and began to recline, looking at the meal fit for a king.

Everyone looked set and ready to eat but were patiently waiting for the prayer.

"Joshua, will you please lead us in prayer over this meal?" Maggie asked him politely.

Joshua nodded in acceptance, asking them all to lock hands with one another, which they did without a fuss. He began his prayer:

"Father, let your name be honored as holy as you give us each day our daily bread, and forgive us our sins, for we also forgive those in debt to us. And do not bring us into temptation."

He added into his words saying to those around;

" *Don't worry about your life, what you will eat or what*

you will drink, or about your body as regards what you will wear. Isn't life more than food and body more than clothing? Look at the birds of the sky. They don't sow or reap or gather into barns, yet your heavenly Father feeds them. Aren't you worth more than they?"

Everyone agreed with Joshua as they all said Amen.

They had just begun to eat when Sarah regaled Maggie about the tale of how her day went at the food bank.

"There were many people today," she said. "We also ran out of food until Joshua found extra trays of food. It was nothing short of a miracle trust me, and I wouldn't have believed it had I been told and not seen it for myself."

Maggie cracked up in laughter by the severe look on Sarah's face.

"God works in mysterious ways my friend," she replied, stuffing some food into her mouth.

"He does," Sarah seconded while casting a stare at Joshua.

"Joshua"... Maggie called out to him, watching him lift his head from his food. "Would you like to open the wine for me please?"

"That would be my pleasure, dear," he replied, as they passed over the wine opener to him and the wine itself.

He placed the wine opener on the cork, twisting it until the metal screw plunged hard and straight down into the cork. With all of his strength, he tanked hard at the cork to get it before it came out with a loud pop. He read the label on the bottle aloud, which read "2000 Montini."

"It must be a sparkling wine looking at the great year," he said to them. "Who would like to wash down their meal with some wine?" he offered.

They raised their glasses to him, while he began to fill the wine glasses and pass them around one after the other.

Maggie stole the chance to have a brief conversation with Sarah on the side, while Joshua shared the wine around.

"I was speaking with the Pastor earlier today, and he is asking the Church members if they wish to do missionary work around Christmas," she informed her friend.

"What sort of missionary work and what location," Sarah paused her meal for details.

"It's in Iraq," Maggie replied.

"Isn't that going to be dangerous? I mean the terrain and hostiles?" Sarah sounded worried.

"I thought so too, but I learned the town we will be visiting has been recovered from the terrorists by the US Military and some Iraqi forces, protecting the village from harm," Maggie laid her fears to calm. "We'd simply be there to assist the kids whose parents are dead or misplaced during the war, while they also have a lovely church there."

"Those children must need food and comfort," Sarah thought.

"I hate to see children suffer," she voiced with a sad tone.

Maggie turned to Joshua, who had been listening to them. "We need someone who knows the bible by heart, and your carpentry skills will come in handy to help build the kids some beds," she said to him.

"That would be lovely, provided I can comfort them in any way I can," Joshua gladly said. "If that be the requirement, then I'd gladly go."

They all nodded in agreement, with glad hearts that they would soon be heading off to provide care and assistance for those in need.

"Let's take a moment to close our eyes and pray," he beckoned them.

> *Jesus, we thank you for this day, Lord and ask that you'd help our group fulfill your teachings. Help us with our missionary journey to Iraq and help the children who lost their parents as well as provide for them to be fed right and remain healthy to the glory of your name."*

They all chimed "Amen" together before Joshua began carving the turkey with a knife. He encouraged them to pass the plates around while Maggie filled them with the side dishes she had prepared.

They soon began to consume their meals, enjoying the food very much. The meal Maggie had prepared was tasty and compelling to the point that some had to order for second rounds.

"I feel so stuffed up my clothes might rip apart if I move too much," Sarah led the line of jokes while feeling pretty filled.

"I think I might decide against eating for the next forty-three days," Joshua added.

"I doubt I can eat anymore," one other guest attested to their claims of being filled already. "I might need to walk it off."

Joshua and the rest laughed hard at the guest, who looked the part on his face, while he stared at his empty plate which had been piled with food just some moments ago.

'Does anyone care for coffee and pie?" Maggie asked with everyone looking at her in surprise. "I also have homemade vanilla ice cream to go with the pies in case anybody is interested."

They all stared at her like she didn't understand the words flying out of her mouth, but they politely declined one after the other, beginning with Sarah.

"Maybe a little while after," Joshua suggested, trying not to waste food, which he didn't consider right as there were those without any to eat.

"Would you all be willing to come with me to the library to play the piano?" She enticed them with a better activity that was sure to spur some of them. "We can sing some holiday songs together."

It was pretty obvious Maggie was somewhat big on Christmas, and Sarah confirmed it with a tease.

"You should see her on Christmas," Sarah teased. "She begins the countdown until Christmas from Thanksgiving." "She thinks about it so much she has a book with all of the days laid out about when and what she intends to cook, amidst other shopping plans."

They all laughed aloud at Sarah's explanation of Maggie's festive yet feverish actions.

"I've never seen anyone so infatuated with Christmas before in my life," she noted.

"That happens to be my favorite time of year," said Joshua. "Maybe it's because someone I know was born on that day."

"Oh? That would be Jesus, isn't it?" Maggie pointed out.

Sarah had begun yawning aloud from where she sat, feeling tired with her eyes threatening to clamp shut at any point in time. It was apparent she intended to draw the night to a close and head off to bed before she spoke.

"It is getting kinda late, and I need to get sleep," she yawned. "I hope to see you again soon."

"Yes, of course," Joshua nodded. "We'll talk about the Missionary trip properly later as well."

The rest of them followed Maggie to the library to enjoy singing Christmas carols. Joshua felt entertained, watching Maggie play the piano. She proved herself to be good at it, while they all sang along and jollied at the moment.

~

He resigned to bed an hour later after helping himself to some of Maggie's delicious pies after his stomach had permitted him to. He walked into his room, feeling exhausted and in need of proper rest but wasn't going to get any rest until he did one more thing.

He slowly went on his knees at the foot of his bed to pray as hard as he could. He called upon his Father regarding the Missionary trip. He was worried because he had no identification card or passport to make the trip, and could be a big problem when the time comes. He wanted assistance in getting things sorted out before he even got there.

His bowed his head, and eyes closed when a big ball of light emerged from above in his room. He knew it was his Father who had come to his call.

"Yeshua, you have my permission to accompany Sarah and the rest to Iraq," He said in a thunderous tone that didn't go past his room.

He was elated to hear that his Father permitted him to go. A few seconds after an ID card, Passport, and Visa appeared on his bed. Also, a nicely fitted well stitched all wool dark gray two-piece suit that any designer tailor would have been jealous to see, a double stitched fitted all white cotton shirt, a pair of black shoes, black socks, leather belt, and requirements tailored especially for him.

"Jeshua, I will give you the personal assignment on reporting to me as regarding the barbaric activities the angels have informed to me which are going on around there," His Father said to him. "This will help bring a viable decision on how best to end the corruption."

The room had just fallen silent when a knock came on his door.

He was in wonder since he wasn't expecting anyone. He walked to the door to unlock it, and standing there in his doorway was Sarah.

"May I come in?" she asked, holding up a shirt. "I failed to give you this," she said, handing Joshua the T-shirt she had in her hand. "The Pastor gave us the shirts, which is what we'll wear on the missionary trip."

It was a yellow shirt with blue lettering on it. The print on it read "Feed the Children Mission," with the abbreviated letters "COTT" which stood for "Chapel of the Transfiguration." Joshua grabbed the shirt from her, gleaming with anxiety.

"I'll try this on right now," he said, looking happy.

Sarah laughed out loud, snatching the shirt back from him to his dismay.

"You're not to put it on now silly," she said comically staring at him. "You're meant to wear it when we're leaving." Joshua gushed with embarrassment almost immediately.

"I just wished to tell you how much I appreciate you are deciding to come with us on this trip," Sarah smiled saying. "This missionary trip means a lot to the church, and I hope we can contribute to the world out there."

"I'm certain God is proud of you for what you do and are willing to do for others," he informed her in an assured tone of voice. "I appreciate your courage and enthusiasm as well, and I feel the same way as you do."

She nodded gently, turning around to head to the door. "Well, it's getting pretty late, and I need to pick up some items for the trip as well as some packing to do."

"Good night, Sarah, I'll see you in the morning."

"Goodnight Joshua," she softly spoke, closing the door behind her for the night.

CHAPTER 8

T he Missionary Trip to Iraq
Upon the morning of their departure, Joshua had picked up his backpack equipped with his essentials, which included the ID, Passport, and VISA his Father had given him. He walked down the stairs after his prayers, meeting Sarah, who had two large suitcases with her.

She looked at him in surprise, staring at the small load he was carrying in comparison to hers.

"Is that all you're taking?" she asked.

He looked at his load, before replying to her; "This is all I have of my worthy possession."

She scoffed slightly, before speaking; "I had difficulties on what clothes to take. I heard it is pretty hot and windy out there."

Joshua nodded as he saw Maggie just coming from the kitchen, bringing out a breakfast tray comprise of tacos and coffee.

"I made you guys a carafe of my special pecan coffee and home-made tacos," she gushed about a job well done. The tacos were hand made of handmade corn tortillas, wrapped individually in aluminum foil to keep them warm." "You have a choice of potatoes and eggs, bacon and eggs or beef chorizo and eggs.

"We're running late," said Sarah. "Perhaps we can eat them on the trip to the airport."

"I'll pour the coffee in to-go cups for you guys," Maggie insisted.

"Joshua, can you help me load my luggage into Maggie's car?" Sarah sought his assistance.

Joshua stepped forward to help her with the luggage, that didn't look as heavy as it was as he lifted them. He frowned as the weight threatened to give him a sprain.

"For crying out loud, these bags are hefty," he pointed out staring at Sarah who was giggling. "What do you have in there?"

"Oh, I'm taking some bibles and study guides with me for the children," she explained.

"Oh, I see," Joshua sighed, picking up the luggage in one hand and using his cane as support for the other.

In one full application of force, he lifted the heavy luggage and placed them inside Maggie's vehicle. He felt exhausted but glad to help.

"Is that all we're taking with us? You need to make sure you don't leave anything behind," he warned.

"Yes, I think I have everything in place," Sarah paused to think it through, before nodding in certainty. "Although I must admit, I do forget things whenever I want to travel or leave home," she chuckled.

Noting that all of their luggage was in the car, Joshua sat in the back, while Sarah sat in the front with Maggie.

"Buckle up guys," Maggie encouraged them with a roar in a comical manner.

Maggie cranked up the car and allowed it to warm up. Sarah

looked at her gas meter, wondering if there was enough gas in the vehicle to convey them to the airport.

"Do you have sufficient gas, Maggie?" she finally asked. "My concern is that we might run out on gas before getting to the airport."

"I was worried of that too," Maggie acknowledged. "So, I got some more last night," she informed them to lay their worries to rest.

"Thank you, Maggie, that's nice of you," Sarah commended.

Joshua grabbed a potato and egg taco from Maggie's bag and carefully unfolded the breakfast taco. He looked at it, saying a brief prayer, before taking a bite, and began to savor the taco. He took a swig of pecan coffee as well, enjoying his meal silently in the back of the car.

"I've never eaten tacos for breakfast before," he confessed to Maggie, who laughed at him from where she was driving. "I must say these are delicious, thank you."

"Damn, I forgot the hot sauce," Sarah sighed. "I told you I always forget something when leaving home," prompting the ladies into a laugh. She sighed before looking at Joshua; "Do you like spicy Mexican food?"

"I've never eaten any Mexican food before," Joshua truthfully replied.

She cast a strange look at him, while Maggie wore the same look with her eyes fixed on the road. They wondered how it was possible someone like him hadn't eaten any Mexican meal before.

"I guess I'll have to take you out to eat some Mexican food soon," she murmured. "There's a new Mexican restaurant not far from here called The Vaquero." "I heard it's pretty good, and we should try it out one day." "That sounds good," said Joshua.

Maggie continued her drive to the airport while Joshua looked out the window. He could see rows and rows of pine trees. The sun was just about easing itself out of the sky as they journeyed on.

"It sounds drab in here," Maggie noted, powering on her CD player that aired a lovely song Sarah seemed to connect with immediately.

Sarah could barely control herself, immediately singing along to the "Amazing Grace Hymn" that was airing through the stereo in the car. Joshua couldn't help but listen diligently to the hymn as well as get impressed by Sarah's sonorous voice. He watched on with a smile tearing apart his lips while she came to an excellent finish as the song ended.

"Bravo! Bravo!" he clapped aloud like a fan who had just watched his favorite creative designer perform. "That was beautiful," he couldn't help but add.

Sarah blushed in an embarrassed manner before struggling to sound appreciative towards his words, "Thank you."

"How did you learn to sing that good?" he inquired, prompting Sarah to look back at him.

"I used to sing it with my grandma," Sarah responded. "She could sing and happened to be a winner of an award on American Idol."

"Is she still around?" Joshua asked further, noting a sour look spread across her face.

"No, she died many years ago," Sarah's voice lingered in pain.

"My condolence," he tendered in sympathy.

"Thank you, but she was a blessed woman all through her life, and died of natural causes," Sarah explained in a happy mood. "She was a hundred and two when she passed away."

Maggie was occupied and focused on her driving while permitting them ample time to discuss and keep busy.

"Wow, she lived a full life," Joshua chimed.

"We just arrived," Maggie finally broke their conversation up. Joshua looked outside the window and saw a row of jet planes of different sizes from the more jumbo framed jets to the smaller ones with propellers on them. Joshua pointed at the small one with the propeller. "Are we taking that one," he said? "Are you being sarcastic?" "I thought you flew on a plane when you came to the USA from Israel," Sarah said? "Don't tell me you came on a prop plane," she said. Not wanting Sarah to know how he arrived here, he quickly interjected to her interrogatory question. "No, not really, but you might say it was like one of those fast jets," he mentioned.

She drove Joshua and Sarah to the passengers' drop off area, before parking the car and pulling the latch on the back trunk of her vehicle. Joshua stepped out first before helping Sarah with her door like a gentleman. Sarah spelled her appreciation before he went to the back of the car to get their luggage and began placing it on the ground.

"I should go get a cart," Sarah suggested, heading off.

Sarah looked around before walking up to an airport attendant, who was standing by, to ask for a cart.

"We have plenty of carts," the nice lady said. "You should go inside; it's where we keep them," she directed Sarah with a point in the right direction. "Do you need any help?"

"Thank you, but we'll be fine," Sarah declined respectfully, before going inside as instructed.

She found a cart as mentioned, and rolled it back to Maggie's vehicle where Joshua began to load the luggage onto the cart immediately. Sarah looked at Maggie in a saddened way, but mostly emotional. She thought about how she was going to miss Church and all of the holiday activities.

"Well, here we are on the day as planned," she said to Maggie. She looked jittery but did well to conceal it while staring at Maggie.

"I'm actually really excited, but on the other hand, I'm also a bit nervous," she confessed.

Maggie chuckled loudly, before walking closer to her; "Don't worry honey, you'll be okay and come to think of it, you have Joshua to comfort you."

Sarah looked at Maggie and smiled.

"I will miss you, Maggie," she confessed with a tight hug for her friend. "Take care, and I will pray for you."

She turned to Joshua, who had just completed his work; "Joshua, you should take good take care of Sarah."

"I definitely will," Joshua replied.

~

Sarah rolled the cart up to the airport attendant where the checking in the unit was, as they bid Maggie goodbye and watched her get back into her car to drive off.

"I'm checking all of these bags," Sarah told the attendant.

The airport attendant looked at Joshua before asking if he intended upon checking in his backpack, to which he declined politely, planning to carry it along with himself. They got things sorted out and headed forward, through the lines, before arriving at the checkpoint. Sarah and Joshua tendered their passports and IDs upon request from the airport attendant, who let them through after checking them.

They walked a little further before arriving at the second checkpoint.

"Could you kindly remove your shoes, take out everything in

your pockets, jackets, and belts and kindly place them on the conveyor belt please," the man spoke in a demanding tone.

They did as they were asked, taking off their belongings and placing them on the belt as asked. Joshua was requested to put his backpack, walking cane and hoodie on the conveyor belt, which he did without a fuss upon instruction.

Sarah went through the metal detector first, getting cleared immediately with no problem, before being asked to pick up her belongings. Joshua was passed to do the same, and he did, hoping nothing would go wrong before the blaring sound of a siren littered the air the moment he stepped through.

The airport security officer came up to Joshua, asking him to stand aside.

"Can you raise your arms and spread your legs apart for us please?" they asked of him.

They swept the metal detector around his body, coming to a stop around his neck where it gave off a sound indicating there was something odd about the area just around his chest. The shrill sound persisted whenever they placed the detector around his chest.

"Can you take off what you have underneath your shirt, please?" the man asked Joshua.

Joshua gently took off the amulet he wore around his neck, handing it over to them.

"That's a stunning amulet you have there," the officer said, gliding his hand over the amulet in admiration.

"Thank you, it was given to me as a gift when I was born," Joshua responded.

The officer continued examining the strange looking amulet in his hands, just before he began feeling a burning sensation on his hand, prompting him to hand it back over to Joshua without delay.

He then resumed a fresh examination of Joshua's body with his metal detector. It was faster this time around, around his arms, legs, and chest region, but the loud beeping sound wouldn't come to an end.

"Sir, can you give me the permission to pat you down?" he asked Joshua with a curious look.

"Yes, you may please," Joshua accepted.

He began patting Joshua down in a manner akin to a police officer searching for illegal substances on a person. He implored the metal detector once more, hearing the object light up in beeps every time, even though he couldn't quite find anything on Joshua with his bare hands. He shook his head in a dumbfounded manner.

"You must be filled with metal or be made of it," the security officer told Joshua. "Are you hiding anything under your skin?"

Joshua gasped immediately, remembering he had failed to tell them exactly what was going on.

"I should have told you I have remnants of metals in my hands and legs that were the result of a work-related incident," he confessed.

"I'm sorry to hear that," the security officer said. "That explains why the detector is making so much fuss, but you're free to pass."

Sarah had been patiently waiting for Joshua, worried sick as well.

"I can't believe they made you go through all that hassle, and now we're about to miss our flight should we not hurry," she complained, glancing at her watch in the process.

"I guess they were just doing their jobs," Joshua said in their defense.

"Come on, let's go before we're late," she beckoned him. Joshua put his shoes and brown hoodie back on before picking up his backpack.

"We better move faster than we are at present," she hurried them forward down the terminal while Joshua stared at the shops, bars, and restaurants around them with amazement.

"This is an interesting merchant market place. Do they collect taxes here?" he asked her.

"That occurs only when you purchase something, except at the duty-free store, where foreigners don't pay taxes," she replied impatiently, but well enough for him to understand.

"That's nice," said Joshua.

"Don't you dare start wandering off on me," Sarah warned him, knowing he could intend upon wanting to see some new things and delay them further.

Joshua seemed to have more questions looming in his head than he can ask entirely. He wanted to know loads of things.

"Are the stores, restaurants, and bars open all day?" he asked again.

"Well, just to a certain point," Sarah looked at him briefly and replied. She could tell he wanted to know, and couldn't fault his inquisitive nature. "The coffee shops and bars are more likely to remain open later than others."

Joshua asked no further question for the time being, as they kept walking through the mammoth crowd walking in opposition to their direction. The crowd made walking quite difficult without having to dodge into someone or apologize for stepping on someone.

"This section is more crowded than the rest," he pointed out. Sarah smiled, knowing it was something normal;

"The coming holidays usually make things this busy," she enlightened him.

They finally arrived at the terminal, where they could see some other people donning the same regalia as theirs.

"I see others in our missionary group came earlier than us," Sarah smiled.

They had begun approaching the group when one of Sarah's Church friends by the name Brad ran over to Sarah to warm her up with a tight bear hug. Brad was a tall, burly white man with short dark hair and wearing a baseball cap, somewhere in his mid 20's, boyishly handsome, brimming with confidence. It was the first time Joshua saw Brad. Joshua focused his eyes on Brad and said to himself, "He is surely a big Jolly guy." Joshua did not meet him earlier since he did not show up for the Baptism dedication.

"Sarah Abrams, I can't tell you how happy I am to see you," he gushed in a smile.

"I should be saying the same as well," Sarah smiled happily, trying to pull herself away from Brad.

Some more people came closer, closing in on Sarah like a hoard of ants while Joshua watched on from where he stood.

"We're pleased to see you. Aren't you excited about this trip?" the Church group asked one another.

"I am," she replied. "I've always wanted to go on a missionary trip to help young children."

She recalled she had been rude not to introduce Joshua all along. She turned to Joshua to get it done.

"Brad and guys, this is Joshua," she said. "He's new to the church, and he is going to help us out on the trip."

Joshua recognized some of the faces from the Baptism dedication earlier. He smiled and greeted them, coming up to them and shaking their hands firmly and proudly saying hello to them all.

"The Pastor told me some of the children at the orphanage are sleeping on the floor, which is one of the reasons Joshua is coming with us on this journey," she explained to the group. "He is skilled at woodworking and can build those bed bunks for them to have a better place to sleep."

Awesome!" Brad exclaimed. He lifted his hand, demanding Joshua give him a high five.

Joshua reciprocated by lifting his hands and giving him a high five.

She had just spoken through when the Pastor came up to them saying; "You guys just got here in time. Did you have any problems getting here?"

Sarah shook her head in reply. "Maggie drove us here, and it was majorly smooth, sailing all the way."

"That's great, well, here, I am going to give you your plane tickets now," Pastor Ed began tendering everyone's plane ticket to them as well as bidding his goodbyes before boarding the plane.

Before boarding the plane, Pastor Ed gathered them all around for a prayer, which was of importance. Everyone gathered into a circle and held hands. They all bowed their heads down and began to recite the prayer.

"*Heavenly Father, please bless everyone that is going on this mission and guide them in every step of their way. Please give them strength and diligence to complete their mission and bring them back safely. Amen.*"

The airline called their group to begin boarding the plane. Sarah and Joshua strolled down the walkway towards the plane. They approached the entrance of the plane, where the waiting flight attendant greeted them.

"Welcome on board," she greeted with a charming smile. Sarah and Joshua both reciprocated, as they passed through the entrance.

Joshua followed Sarah as they walked the narrow aisle of the plane, looking at the seat numbers. She looked at her ticket meticulously with a sight of frustration.

"A bit further down," she instructed Joshua to look for his number on the seat.

They walked much further down the aisle and Joshua never having been on an airplane before found the interior quite interesting. "These leather chairs look quite comfortable." "I believe I will take a nap when I sit down." "Here are our seats, said Sarah, and from the looks of it, you're sitting next to me," she giggled. "It is great, isn't it, and we can keep each other company."

Sarah opened the overhead compartment and put her carry-on inside. Joshua handed his backpack and came to Sarah, who kept them close to hers as well. Joshua took the seat next to the aisle, and Sarah took the seat in the middle. Brad came up to them, looking at his ticket in the process.

"Hello, it seems I got myself the window seat," he chuckled.

"You're a lucky man," Sarah congratulated him.

Joshua pulled himself back to give Brad spare room so he could get by, but his large thick legs brushed against his knees, sending a radiating pain throughout his legs. He cringed and frowned in pain. Sarah had just noticed it, informing Brad to be careful.

"He has an injury, and you need to be careful about his leg," she informed Brad.

"I'm so sorry," said Brad, who then walked by Sarah and almost fell on her.

He was pretty clumsy from the looks of it, and Joshua had to caution him to watch where he was going, before hurting Sarah.

"These seats are so tight, and I'm a huge guy," he complained his case, before finally sitting down.

The pilot activated the "fasten your seat belt" light just before a bell rang. The flight attendant went up and down the plane and began to close the carry-on compartments as expected, to avoid letting any belongings fall out. The passengers immediately put their seat belts on.

The captain of the plane made another announcement just a few moments after they had gotten on their seat belts.

"Hello, this is John Hoover, and I say welcome to Flight 777," He was a husky sounding man that obeyed protocol. "We're well fueled up, and we will be taking off shortly with clear skies and perfect visibility."

It was fun for Joshua who listened tentatively "There are other planes on the runway at the moment, but we will be cleared to fly soon enough," he finally ended his speech.

The flight attendant stood in the middle of the row of the plane and began to show the emergency procedures. Joshua stared at the lady closest to him and watched with curiosity. The flight attendant pointed out the emergency exits. She then unfolded a yellow life preserver vest and secured the vest belt with a click. She instructed everyone that if the plane was to crash into the water, once they were outside the plane, to pull down on the red cord and watch the vest blow up.

"If that failed, you could blow into the plastic tube," she said. Joshua mumbled; "Noah and his people could have used one of those."

She further instructed them on the course of action to take should the air mask fall on the cabin floor, but Joshua had taken a quick peek at Sarah to know if she was listening. He found her looking a bit tense. He wondered why.

"Aren't you interested in what the flight attendant is saying?" he asked her.

"I've heard it many times and know it by heart already," Sarah shook her head saying.

"Why are you upset?" he asked, switching to another topic? "Is anything wrong?"

"Every time I fly, the pressure in the cabin makes my earache and gives me a headache," she whispered, trying not to voice out loud. "I have sensitive ears."

"I will pray for you to have no such symptoms; hence," Joshua said to her with a nod.

"Thanks, Joshua, I hope so too, but it always occurs on every flight I have taken," she explained.

The Captain of the airplane came on the speaker again; "Folks sorry for the delay. We are scheduled as the third to take off behind the other planes, but we should take off soon."

Brad looked at Joshua and Sarah briefly with a smile, before looking back out the window.

"I must confess I'm the person least looking forward to this flight taking off," Sarah sounded in worry.

"Everything will work out just fine, and you need not worry yourself," Joshua did his best to calm her.

The Captain spoke aloud again on the speakers, informing them they were about to take off, and the necessity to have their seat belts on. The "fasten your seat belt" light began blinking as well as the "no smoking" sign. Once again, the Captain instructed the flight attendants to fasten their seat belts.

"We are available for takeoff," he said before the roaring of the jet engines could be heard.

Upon hearing them take off, Sarah began to grind her teeth and jitter. The plane made progress, going faster with each passing second. In a matter of some more seconds, the nose of the plane lifted upward, and the thrust pushed everyone back against their seat. The airplane took off into the sky and was in the air in minutes before the Captain moved the plane into a horizontal position.

The Captain finally informed them they were flying above 40,000 feet at the time. He welcomed them to move about the cabin as they pleased. Sarah strangely stared at Joshua, having opened her eyes after shutting them in fear earlier.

"That's strange," she softly stated.

"What is?" Joshua asked, staring right back at her.

"For the first time, I don't feel the pressure in my ears, and I don't have a headache during a flight or take off," she smiled. Not knowing Joshua was behind manipulating the pressure sensitivity of the cabin, she was pleased.

"Perhaps the airline engineers figured out a way to pressurize the cabin correctly," said Joshua.

∼

Their flight extended into the night, during which the passengers had begun falling asleep including Sarah. Joshua fell asleep last, easing into it about an hour after Sarah. After an hour into his sleep, the airplane started to bob the passengers in the cabin, jolting them to awaken with worry. The passengers immediately began waking up one after the other in quick response and at an alarming rate.

The seat belt light came on before the pilot began speaking; "Don't worry folks, we're simply going through some heavy turbulence, but should stabilize soon."

He was wrong. The turbulence became worse as the passengers could very well take note of the drastic turn of events through the window with flashes of accompanying light thunder. Brad looked outside the window shaking his head profusely in acknowledgment of the problem at hand.

"It doesn't seem good," he said with a heavy heart.

The other passengers had begun to panic as well. The paranoia in the cabin had heightened tremendously since the captain tried calming them down.

"We're all going to die! We're going to die!" someone stood up to yell aloud and further worsen the scenario.

Sarah was scared out of her wits, while Joshua sleeps soundly like a baby without any worry of what was going on. He murmured like a man dreaming in his sleep, as images of the time he was with his disciples, flashed through his thoughts in slumber. He dreamed of the time when they were in a boat crossing the Sea of Galilee, and they were all caught in a thunderstorm.

Sarah couldn't help herself anymore, as she grabbed tightly onto Joshua's arm, while in the process, shaking him hard until he woke up from his sleep. Joshua woke up looking startled by the state of things, while others were screaming and causing a disturbing stir in the atmosphere on the plane which had been silent before he slept.

"Joshua, wake up, we're going through a bad thunderstorm," she informed him. "I'm scared and don't think it will stop."

Joshua looked at her like she was disturbing herself over what she shouldn't, before getting up and staring out the window into the menacing thunderstorm; He yelled, "Be still!"

His words met with the thunderstorm, and it dissipated immediately. Without the turbulence ramming hard against its wings in an unsettling manner, the plane became still. The passengers calmed themselves immediately, checking their seat belts with their hearts racing hard underneath their chests.

He turned over to Sarah slowly, casting her a look of inquiry."
Why are you fearful?" he asked. "Do you have not your faith any
longer?"

He returned into his seat, just about the time the pilot
announced that the storm had dissipated, before turning off the
"fasten your seat-belt" sign as they all clapped aloud for the next few
seconds, and began easing themselves back to sleep.

CHAPTER 9

A rrival in Iraq
The plane finally began its descent towards Baghdad
international airport as the pilot informed the passengers
of their arrival.

"Folks we're about to land in Baghdad and the weather today is
sunny," he sounded like a glad man bringing the journey to an end.
"We thank you for flying with us; we will be landing shortly."

The "fasten your seat belt" light had just come on with a beep
while Brad opened the sliding window panel to take a good look
outside the plane.

"Take a look at this," he said, prompting Sarah and Joshua to turn
their heads to look in the direction of the window.

All they could see were sand dunes and some white buildings.
The plane got closer to the ground with each passing fraction of a
second, before finally meeting its wheels with the tarmac and those
aboard the plane could well hear a screeching sound.

The airplane cabin bobbed up as the Captain let the wing of the plane drop.

The inertia of the landing threw the passengers forward, pressing them against their seat belts. The airplane finally came to a screaming halt, bringing the passengers relief that they had landed.

"Thank the good, gracious Lord," Sarah gladly said.

"Amen to that," seconded Brad.

The plane moved closer to the hangers where a man with two red flashlights guided the Captain forward. The plane stopped, and the seat belt lights went off immediately. The passengers heard a loud bump against the airplane; it was the stairs getting attached to the outside of the door. The door opened up, and the passengers opened the overhead bins and began to remove their carry-ons.

The passengers lined up one after the other as they began to vacate the airplane. As they walked down the metal stairs, they detected an odor of burnt petrol. The light breeze and salty air made their lips feel parched. Upon setting their feet on the ground, they began to walk towards the building in sight. The airport servicemen drove up to the plane with their flatbed trucks and opened the plane's luggage compartment and began to bring down the luggage.

The passengers were directed through the lines to present themselves to the immigration officers. Joshua had begun gathering some attention with eyes cast upon him in strange looks because of his beard and long hair.

One immigration officer and two security personnel approached them, keeping their gaze on him like he was a threat.

"Hello sir, may we have a word or two with you?" the first of the three asked politely.

Joshua complied, engaging them without a fuss.

"Where are you from sir, and do you have a family here?" the other man asked in a simultaneous speaking manner.

He replied them honestly, before providing them the permission to go through his things after they had asked. They searched his backpack and found a shirt, undergarments, his two-piece suit folded nicely in a roll and other necessities. They opened his passport and noticed his birthplace was Israel with a weird look crossing their faces.

"So you were born in Israel?" asked the third immigration officer.

"Yes, I was born in Israel," Joshua attested. "I was born in Bethlehem but immigrated to the USA."

"What is your business here, sir?" the first guy asked all over again like they were taking turns.

Joshua fixed his eyes on the immigration and security officers, and their eyes twitched as if they had just received a message through Telepathy. "I'm with the Church Mission here to build beds for the orphaned children," he explained.

They stared at his shirt for a few seconds, before leaving him be without any further questions.

"Very well, that is fine, and you can move on," they said to him.

He walked away; noticing that it was Sarah's turn to be interviewed by the immigration officers. She walked toward them diligently without any worry on her face. The immigration officers smiled and stared at her noticing how beautiful she was. They briefly lost their train of thought and began to fix their eyes on her light blonde hair, fair skin, and the most particularly striking blue eyes.

"Where are you going?" they asked.

Sarah informed them of their mission to help the children's orphanage in Bartella and how they hoped to keep the kids alive and in proper sustenance even after they left. The officer smiled upon hearing the name of the place she had called.

"Bartella! That's my home town," he sighed before lighting with a smile.

"I'm glad to hear that from you," Sarah spoke.

"Children suffer tremendously around that area," he told her. "Just a warning though, be careful and don't wander outside of the town, or you might get yourself in trouble by getting your head chopped off or getting burned at stake."

"We have a guide who works for the orphanage, and he will take us there," Sarah assured him of her intent not to wander off.

"That's good to know, you may leave now," he said with a wave.

~

Sarah joined Joshua before heading towards the luggage claim area to pick up their luggage. When they arrived there, they saw a man with dark sunglasses, a dark mustache, and salted pepper color hair. He wore a gray color suit, with a white shirt and a purple necktie. He was carrying a sign that read "Sarah and Joshua COTT" in his hands held just around his chest.

They approached him seeing their church's abbreviation and their names on his sign.

"Hello, I'm Tariq," he said upon seeing they had taken an interest in what he held in his hands. "You must be Sarah and Joshua," he extended his hand while they nodded. "Yes, we are," said Sarah. "It's nice to meet you. I will be your guide to take you to the church's orphanage."

Joshua looked at Sarah briefly before turning back to him.

"Come with me please," Tariq said. "There will be a van coming soon to pick the others."

He picked up their bags individually from the floor next to the baggage conveyor belt and placed them on a cart he brought with him. "Follow me," he said. He pushed the cart with ease and went through the airport building sliding doors, leading them toward the outside passenger pick up area. "This is my minivan," he said. He proudly presented it to them as it was his only prized possession.

Sarah couldn't help but feel they were getting some special treatment, which she whispered to Joshua.

"I guess they made us leaders of the missionary," Joshua replied with a smile.

Joshua took note of the windows on Tariq's van that was heavily tinted. Tariq opened the door and let them in. Sarah and Joshua sat down in the van, noticing the beige color leather-covered seats and helped themselves with their seat belts.

Tariq gave Sarah a black Hijab. "This is your head cover, which you must wear at all times here," he warned her. "All women wear these here as a symbol of modesty and privacy."

Sarah had no problem with it, but she wanted to know what would happen if she refuses to wear it. Her question turned Tariq's face into a more serious looking one.

"If you don't wear it, someone will hit you on the side of your head with a stick," he replied. "You will have to wear this veil when you go to any public places."

Sarah looked straight at it and then turned to Joshua. "I wasn't expecting this, but I guess I have no choice but to go ahead with it for my safety," she sighed.

Sarah began placing the head cover and veil slowly over her head. She wasn't feeling comfortable in the compulsory fashion and wondered if she had to make use of it every blessed day and time, which would be nothing but trouble for her.

"Do I need to wear this when I sleep as well, Tariq?" she was forced to ask.

"No, you don't, only when you are outside; without it, you might get attacked physically for indecency," he replied.

Sarah looked at Joshua with frustration showing Joshua how uncomfortable it was. Joshua smiled.

"It's just temporary," he said to her to calm her down.

Tariq started the car, but it coughed out and refused to start. The engine sounded as though it was choking. He attempted it again for the second time, but it gave the same sound as before and refused to come alive. He looked startled and frustrated in equal portions.

"I don't know what's going on," he scratched his head, saying.

"It worked just some hours ago when I drove here."

Joshua leaned towards the front seat saying; "Let me help you, Tariq, I have some working knowledge about car engines."

Joshua came out of the car where Tariq had opened the hood for him to have a look. Joshua laid his finger on the battery, prompting some sparks to flash wildly. He instructed Tariq to go ahead to give it one more try, which he did duly and to his surprise, the car kicked to life.

Tariq jumped in his seat, joyously as he revved up the car's engine.

"What did you do to get it started?" asked Tariq as he got back out to close the hood.

"I simply adjusted the battery cable a bit," he shrugged his shoulders.

Tariq looked at Sarah saying; "You brought a fine man here with you," accompanying his words with a chuckle.

"Yes, I did," said Sarah. "He is very handy in things, and knows how to build furniture, but I wasn't aware he was also mechanically inclined."

"He will help us a lot at the orphanage," Tariq said, driving off. They drove for miles, seeing nothing but desert sand, dried ground cover, rocks, and boulders. Nothing was out of the ordinary until a caravan of camels passed by them on the side of the road.

Tariq commented; "They are merchants taking their goods to the market," before looking through his rearview mirror to see a truck approaching him.

The truck behind them had a flatbed, covered with canvas and carrying a load but could not be seen. The driver of the truck was moving at a fast rate, approaching Tariq's car, getting pretty close enough to tailgate him in the process.

Tariq honked his horn, flashing his lights in the process to avert the driver away, before shaking his head and letting him pass.

"They're always in a hurry off somewhere," he sighed. "Most times, they end up in accidents, which would be the lesson they come to learn too late after it occurs about patience and not speeding."

Along the way, they drove past a caravan of armed troops, providing Joshua with insight into the situation of things.

"They are the Iraqi special forces," Tariq pointed out. "They liberated the town of Bartella where we are going, which is an ancient Christian Iraqi town."

"How far is it from the main war zone?" Joshua inquired. "That's thirteen miles east of Bartella in a place called Mosul where they're trying to liberate from the war as well as from the terrorists," Tariq responded. "Over 100 children were discovered hiding among the buildings. They were kidnapped and held in Mosul's orphanage."

Sarah gasped in horror. The idea of kids subjected to so much trauma struck her as inhumane. She couldn't begin to picture that.

"Their parents died fighting while the terrorists warred against them, and in the process, they made an effort to destroy the church by burning crosses and tearing the paintings and images we had in the church," Tariq narrated some more heartbreaking experiences they faced with the terrorists in their fight for liberation. "You can still see bullet holes on the columns and church pews before the town people got together and decided to repair it although it isn't the same as it used to be."

They had just driven past the church, which Tariq pointed out to them.

"I'll take you there later, but we need to visit the orphanage first," he noted. "It's just down the street."

Tariq sped down the road, quickening their arrival at the orphanage.

The orphanage was an old white stucco square building with a red tile roof and very few windows. Wrought iron bars covered the windows and each coated with thick paint and laking rust. The building stucco walls were riddled with bullet holes and was peeling. In the front were two large plain wooden doors with wrought iron handles on them. As Tariq approached the orphanage, he honked his horn to notify of their arrival, and a woman peeked through the window curiously watching them as they drove up. A curvy, short height, middle age woman burst through the front doors and came running toward their car.

She wore a black hijab with white daisy print and diamond sequence. She had a large bony nose, light skin, rosy red cheeks and spoke with a Middle Eastern accent. She introduced herself upon arrival to them as the caretaker of the orphanage.

"Hello, my name is Saadia, and I'm pleased to welcome you to Bartella," she grinned. She looked into the minivan, noting it was just Sarah and Joshua in it. "Where are the others?" she asked immediately? "They should be here soon," Sarah assured her.

Saadia nodded, before speaking to Sarah; "We're so glad you came in time because we just acquired two new children whose parents are nowhere to be found."

"They must be frightened and in need of comfort," Sarah pointed out.

"Yes, indeed, they have no family anymore, and we're not sure how long they will grieve," she said. "We hope that someday we can place them with a family," Saadia concluded. "Come with me," she encouraged them.

Joshua had ventured toward getting their luggage when Saadia stopped him.

"You need not worry about your luggage, Tariq will get them in for you," Saadia said to him. "Just come with me. It's the children's lunchtime at the moment."

"They must be frightened and in need of comfort," Sarah pointed out.

Saadia led them to the foyer, where there was a huge ornamental red and black carpet with geometric diamond patterns on it. The walls were smeared with stucco and had blue motifs painted on the surfaces. The ceilings had beaded rustic wood. The door had wooden arches with rivets in them. They took a moment to admire the environment before Saadia led them further into another room.

Inside the main room, there were two large wooden hands carved doors bearing a round circular motif with a floral pattern. The doors had two large brass handles. Saadia pulled the large wooden doors apart to expose a lightly dimmed room. In the large room, there were two rows of wooden tables and benches on which the children were sitting. They all wore similar garments, plain white cotton pants, and white cotton shirts. The boys wore white taqiyah hats while the older girls had burqas.

Upon their entry, they looked right at Sarah and Joshua without casting a smile off of their lips. They seemed rather thin and fragile as they waited patiently for their meals. Saadia had deemed it necessary to introduce their guests.

"Children may I have your attention please?" she asked of them, watching them stare at her. "This is Sarah and Joshua, and they are from a Christian church in America and are here to help you," she explained to the listening children. "Others will come soon, and I'll introduce them to you later as well."

Some of Saadia's helpers came in with several large pots of lentil soup and some bread, after her introduction.

"That is all we have to feed the children for today," Saadia said broken-heartedly. "Supplies are coming and should be here anytime soon," she continued, giving Sarah a pot and asking her to help fill the children's empty bowls with soup.

Joshua task was to handle out the trays of bread to the kids. Joshua took the tray closest to him to begin with first, handing each child a piece of bread as they approached in an orderly manner. The children stared at Joshua as though they were curious about him. However, they were starving as he muttered words they could barely understand, thereby, they paid little attention to his words, but rather to the food he had to offer them.

Joshua distributed all of the portions he had with him and then took some time to watch Sarah pour the soup into the children's bowls as Saadia poured water into the children's cups. After getting through with his task, he took place at the table and stared at the children eating the bread while reminiscing about his Passover with his disciples.

~

He was sharing bread and cup with them in remembrance of his last night with his disciples. It is a solemn and holy night to consider all that had happened within the final hours before the guards arrested him and took him away. Joshua had been sitting at the head of the table with his disciples by his side when he had said;

"I assure you that one of you will betray me," in a profoundly distressed tone.

He could recall each one begins to say to him, "Surely not I. Lord," before he replied; "The one who dips his hand with me in the bowl will betray me."

He could recall taking a large loaf of wheat bread and lifting the bread above his head and breaking the bread in half after he had blessed it, before saying unto them;

"Take and eat it, for this is my body given to you, so for this day you will always remember me," before taking up the cup of wine next which he blessed and said; "Drink from it, all of you, for this is my blood that establishes the covenant which is shed for many for the forgiveness of sins."

He engrossed his thoughts about times past when Sarah nudged him to wake up.

"Wake up, Joshua!" she yelled, making him struggle to regain himself.

"Did I doze off?" he asked, unsure if he had.

"You must be tired because you were dozing already," she told him. "Saadia asked if you could build two beds for the two kids who just came in."

"The two kids who just came in that she told us about?" Joshua asked again.

"Yes, they were sleeping on the floor since they came and needed a proper bed," Sarah said.

"I'll gather wood and begin work on it right away," he said to Sarah, just about the time Saadia stepped back into the room.

"I'll show you where you can work in an area behind the orphanage that was once used as the stables," "There you'll find saws, hammers, and nails, but it's already too late to start on them right now, and you both look exhausted."

She walked them off to their rooms afterward.

"We only have mattresses on the floors to sleep on for now," she said to them.

"If I have some wood left after the work, I'll build some bed frames for those mattresses," Joshua said.

Sarah was feeling grungy and in need of a shower, asking Saadia if there was one she could use. Unfortunately, they had no hot water.

Saadia informed Sarah of the broken water, and the pipes make a loud noise."Perhaps Joshua can fix it."

"Well, it looks like we're about to rough it out," Sarah smiled. "I will take a shower in the morning," Joshua noted his intent to remain calm till morning the way he was. "It's too cold for me."

Saadia walked towards Sarah. "We have clean towels on the shelves next to the showers and one water closet next to it, and in case you need anything, such as soap, shampoo or toilet paper lets me know."

Sarah bid Saadia goodnight with appreciative words for her kindness.

"I'll put the children to bed right now, and perhaps tomorrow you can tell them a bed night story," Saadia said before leaving the room.

Sarah looked over to Joshua with a sigh.

"Missionary work has never been easy, and most people mistake it for vacation until they arrive," she sighed.

"You should cast all your anxieties on the Lord, because he will always take care of you," Joshua encouraged her.

"You're right Joshua," she sighed. "Well, I'm about to take my cold shower now."

Joshua walked out toward his room. "If you need anything, I'll be in my room," he said to her.

"Goodnight Joshua," Sarah greeted.

∼

Sarah grabbed her toiletries, slippers, and pajamas and walked down the dimly lit hallway leading to where the shower was situated. It was a tiny shower stall, and she had to pull the plastic blue shower curtains to reveal the stall. The pattern on the walls and floor have an Islamic geometric design pattern. The elements were well combined, duplicated, interlaced, and arranged in intricate combinations. The faucet and shower head were all made of heavy stainless steel and a bit worn.

Sarah looked around, wishing the bathroom had a heated, hot tub.

"Perhaps, I can get Joshua to build me one," she shrugged before recalling she was about to have a cold bath. "I'll quickly jump into the cold water and dream of being inside a hot tub."

She turned both faucets, and the pipes began to make a loud banging sound. Sarah got startled while impatiently waiting for the water to come out. As the water began to emerge from the shower head, she ran her hands under the low flow shower head to ascertain its temperature.

"Yeah, it's freaking cold," she gathered.

She took her clothes off, quickly running under the shower. "Oh, my God! It's colder than I thought," she acknowledged. Then, she grabbed the soap bar and rubbed it against her body, before taking the shampoo and conditioner and dumping them both onto her hair and scrubbing it through hard, before rinsing it off quickly.

She finally shut the faucets noting she couldn't take the cold anymore. She couldn't risk getting hypothermia. Sarah wrapped her towel around her head and put on her woolen pajamas. She walked back to her dimly lit room and shut the door behind her gently heading over to where her bag was, she took out one of the bibles out from her suitcase and sat at the edge of her bed, placing the Bible on the nightstand and began reading it. She then stood up and pulled the woolen bed covers up and laid down on the bed. The bed reeked a musty odor. As she tossed and turned to find that perfect sleeping position, the bed began to make creaking noises. The pillow was hard, and she felt like she was laying her head on a bag of sand. The mattress was excessively firm, and it was awkward for her, yet she couldn't have cared less since she was too worn out to even think about considering it.

After an hour of observing her quiet time, she decided to turn off the lights, and she began to doze off.

In the middle of the night, the sound of a motor awakened

Sarah. The room became colder than it was before she slept, and she pulled the covers up towards her to gain some needed warmth. She could hear the sound of glass shattering from a distance.

"Perhaps Saadia was up, and she had dropped a glass," she thought.

Her thought got distorted as she heard the roaring sound of a motorcycle in the distance, prompting her to wonder who was making the sound. She got startled and decided to sit up. Upon sitting up, by the foot of her bed, she could see a man on a motorcycle staring right back at her.

The man had a brown jacket on with a scarf around his neck and kaffiyeh on his head. He had a beard and long hair as well. He wore a belt around him with tubes hanging down from it. He cast a deep stare at Sarah before laughing out loud and hard in an intimidating manner.

"All you infidels will come to your end and die," he snarled in an evil grin that sent some amount of shivers down Sarah's spine.

Sarah couldn't help but let out a scream immediately as he turned his motorcycle and faced the wall in the room. He revved up the motor and drove towards the wall as fast as he could. No sooner than he rushed through the wall, he disappeared immediately.

Sarah could feel her chest pounding hard, and her throat swelling with worrisome lumps within it.

"I must have seen a ghost," she thought to herself. "Joshua! Joshua!"

Her yells called the man into the room as fast as his legs could carry him, while completely neglecting his cane to heed her cry for help. He helped her switch on the light that was by the entrance of the door.

"What is wrong, Sarah?" he asked, sounding out of breath. Sarah ran up to Joshua and hugged him tightly as she had never done before. She was shaking badly.

"I think I just saw a ghost," she recalled.

"Did you say you saw a ghost?" he asked her again to be sure he had heard right.

"Yes, and he was driving a motorcycle," she narrated with conviction.

Joshua didn't buy it, shaking his head gently; "Perhaps you had a bad dream," he said to her.

"No, it was not some dream, trust me, I heard a clash like a glass had been broken. The motorcycle drove by me and disappeared into the wall," Sarah explained in reasonable detail, staring into his eyes for him to believe her. "It was a man wearing a scarf, kaffiyeh and a brown jacket."

"I need you to calm down, Sarah," Joshua said. "You had a long day, and you need to have a rest now because I must confess, I've never seen a ghost before, and I don't think you'll be seeing more motorcycles."

"I hope not," said the terrified looking Sarah.

～

The following morning, Saadia prepared breakfast for Sarah and Joshua. She made them scrambled eggs, feta cheese, homemade pita bread, and tea. Sarah and Joshua sat down to speak with her.

"I'm just worried about the others in our church group. They were expected to arrive last night," Sarah said in a saddened tone.

"I spoke with Tariq," said Saadia "I learned that the roadblocks delayed their delayed their arrival."

"I hope they get here soon," she voiced her worries aloud; with a frown lining her face in the process.

"Don't worry," said Saadia. "They are in good hands, and I'm sure Tariq will bring them here soon. Did you get a lovely night sleep?"

"I didn't, but I'm sure Joshua did," Sarah replied.

"What happened my dear?" Saadia sounded worried.

"I heard noises and saw a ghost in my room," Sarah explained to her.

"This is an old place, and occasionally, I hear some noises, but I've never seen a ghost," Saadia informed her. "I slept well last night and didn't hear a thing though but the cry of the rooster right before sun up."

"Trust me; I told you what I saw" Sarah sighed. "From the looked of it, it seems you'd never believe me even if I went on to explain."

"Perhaps you had a bad dream, my dear. It's your first day here, and you were exhausted and stressed out," Saadia tried to calm her down. "Come to the parlor, and let's sit there to talk, relax, eat, and drink more tea."

"Joshua, would you like to start on the children's beds?" Sarah reminded him of the work at hand.

"I'd love to," he confirmed. "Show me where I need to go." He turned to Saadia to ask her.

"Come over here to the window, let me show you," Saadia waved him over to her.

Saadia pointed out the window to him, showing him the way which Joshua took to, heading through the back door and over to the stables. He opened two large wooden doors before walking in. There he found a large table to work on and by the side was a pile of wood, with pieces dry wood enough to allow him to build bunk beds.

On the opposite side of the table, there were a few horse stall divided by a wooden post. Mounds of hay laid on the floor. Leather horses harness hung on each post. The wooden slats were coming off the walls while there was a hole in the roof of the stables. There were shelves on the walls with metal buckets. Joshua took one to throw his nails.

He saw remnants of barley and alfalfa in the buckets and turned one over to drop whatever pieces were in it to the ground. He placed the bucket on the table and took a long wooden board and began to sand it down. While sanding it down, he stared at one of the stalls and reminisced about the day he was born.

$$\sim$$

He saw his mother Mary and Joseph who was right by his side. He was laying on Joseph's tallit, a Hebrew prayer shawl, and beneath it was a feeding trough full of hay. He was a baby crying, having just come out of his mother's womb. A bright light shone through the roof, and he heard Mary in joyous tone saying;

"Oh, my Emmanuel" as three wise men walked in to see him who had been told by the Angels of his presence and wanted to know if it was true.

They walked in and stared at the child with curiosity before leaving abruptly to tell the nations of his birth. He was the symbol and representative of the human life he would lead. He could see from there and then that his life did not fall within the privileged luxury, but he remained appreciative of who he was and what he was about to do for all humankind.

He could see everything now, from the day he came into the world to fulfill promises, to the life of persecution and humility he received. Nonetheless, that was his father's will, and he remained without worry that it had come to be as such. He could see and relive the experiences of the 8th day when he was circumcised and became known as Jeshua (Jesus).

He had been absent minded when Sarah walked through the doors and interrupted his thoughts while she had a tray in her hand.

"I thought you might be hungry, so I brought you something to eat and drink," she spoke in a considerate tone as she walked closer. "We made some tuna fish and egg sandwiches, and we cut up some oranges as well."

"Thank you, Sarah," said Joshua. "How are the kids doing?" he asked.

"The children have anxiety and depression because they miss their parents," she replied to him with a sad face. "It's going to take a lot to comfort them."

"Those who mourn are blessed, for they are comforted," Joshua said to her. "I'll finish these beds before sundown, and they can sleep in them comfortably through the night."

"I hope they have enough mattresses, if not we'll have to fill bags of hay for them to lie down on," Sarah explained.

Joshua finally got through with his work, taking the pieces he had assembled towards the orphaned children's room where some of the children slept on the floor, and he began to nail them together. A child by the name Alima stood up from the floor and stared at Joshua. Alima was ten years of age. Her hair was straight and chestnut color, her eyes blue, her face was round, her skin was light, and she had a little button nose. "Is that a bed for me?" she asked in a tiny, curious voice.

"As soon as I'm done putting it together, it could be yours." Joshua smiled at her.

She smiled back at him, holding her hands behind her back as she swung her body joyfully. "In our home, I had many brothers and sisters, and we barely had enough beds to sleep in, so I shared the bed with my sister."

"Well, now you'll have your bed and be as comfortable as possible," Joshua said to her.

She stared at him briefly before asking; "Where did you learn to build beds?"

Joshua took a moment to pause, staring up into her eyes; "Well, I had a good teacher," he said.

"Who was your teacher?" the inquisitive little bee asked.

"His name was Joseph," he replied, returning his focus to his work.

"Was he your father?" she remained relentless in getting enough information as possible from him.

"You can say he was my stepfather," Joshua muttered.

"Was your father killed like mine?" she continued.

He was getting pretty weary of the questions but kept his focus partly on the work and the girl.

"Not quite, but I still feel him with me all the time," he told the little girl.

Alima smiled and said; "It's nice you had two fathers." Joshua shook his head in confusion, thinking about explaining the situation of things about his parents to the girl. She seemed rather tired and unwilling to listen, though.

"You need not worry," she said to him with a smile across her face. "I understand quite well," she added before running off. Joshua shook his head, noting how complicated children were. He went ahead to finish the bunk bed he was building, setting them next to the others afterward. In contrast to the other bunk beds present, his work depicted better craftsmanship than the others.

The bed was sturdier than the rest.

"Perhaps tomorrow I'll fix the other ones," he thought to himself.

Saadia came in with the children shortly afterward.

"It's past their bedtime, and we need to get to the market to replenish the food supplies," she said.

He nodded and walked off to make preparations for the following morning.

~

Morning came as expected, with the arrival of the rest from the airport. The crew included Brad, Carla, Ed, and Samantha as they got out of the van in order. They walked up towards the orphanage and helped themselves in, looking tired and exhausted from their trip and delay.

"Is anyone home," Brad called out.

Saadia had been sitting at the table with Sarah and Joshua when they heard a voice across the room. They had just finished feeding the children with some flatbread and Gaymer Wa Dibis, a thick, creamy, white cream made with buffalo milk.

"I think I just heard someone's voice coming from outside," Saadia noted. "Let me go and see who they are. They most likely could be our church group, which is way long overdue."

Saadia went out to greet them.

"Hello, my name is Saadia, and I'm the caretaker of this orphanage," she humbly said.

"Hello, Saadia, I'm Brad, this is Ed, Carla, and Samantha." "Nice to meet you. I cannot tell you how happy I am that you.

all came to assist us," Saadia chimed with a gladdened smile.

"Sarah and Joshua are here eating breakfast. Would you like to join us?" she offered.

"We sure can use a good cup of coffee," Ed said, smiling while rubbing his hands together.

"Please forgive me, but we don't have any coffee right now, just tea," Saadia sadly said. "Come with me please; she beckoned on them."

They followed as asked, heading towards the kitchen while Brad talked to Saadia about their journey from the airport to the orphanage.

"There were roadblocks on our way here, which delayed our arrival," he explained.

"That happens sometimes," Saadia attested to what he said. "They do it to keep the terrorists in check and prevent them from infiltrating the town."

"They informed me about that," Brad attested to it as well.

They arrived at the kitchen where Sarah and Joshua looked surprised to see them. They ran toward them, to hug them while sharing their experiences coming over.

"We had to spend the entire night in the van on our way out here," Ed explained with a harsh tone. "It was dark, but we could hear the firing of rockets."

"I spotted a meteor or some bright light some nights ago, and it was quite cool," Samantha narrated her part.

"Well, I'm glad you made it here," Sarah sounded. "Sit down, please. I bet you're exhausted."

"It's not every day you sleep within a packed van while some of our fellow church group snores," Samantha joked, nudging Brad, and staring at Ed.

"Where are the children?" Brad inquired.

"We just fed them breakfast, and they are playing now," Saadia replied. "Also, Joshua just finished building new bunk beds, and I was thinking of going to the chicken roost to gather feathers to make a few extra pillows for the children."

Brad inspected the kitchen, rummaging around like a hungry bear, taking note to see if there was any food left over since he had only eaten a small falafel pita sandwich for breakfast that he had bought from a road vendor on his way to the orphanage. He looked over at Joshua who seemed to have adjusted well since he arrived, with no bothered look on his face. "Are you ok Brother"? "Yes, I am ok, just a bit tired," Joshua replied. "I was working on building bunk beds for the children last night." "Cool, I'd like to see them," said Brad.

"We need to go to the Central Market today to buy some food and pick up some supplies," Saadia continued. "I'd suggest you guys stay here and rest."

"Yes, you can become acquainted with the children afterward," Sarah interrupted. "They're nice kids."

"That sounds like a lovely plan," Brad agreed.

CHAPTER 10

The Market Place

Tariq got the minivan ready for them, driving to a halt just outside the orphanage. He had made sure to check the minivan and fill the tank with gas the night before, as well as checking the oil and fluid levels since it would be dangerous to stop in the middle of the road for those provisions. Tariq opened the doors of the minivan for Sarah and Joshua to come in. Without their expectation, Alima ran up to Joshua pleading for them to take her with them.

"Please, take me with you. Please, I've never been to the market," Alima pleaded. "I want to know what they sell there."

"It may not be prudent for a young little princess like you, dear," Sarah turned her down.

"Oh, please, please," she pleaded on and on.

Saadia was standing outside, staring at them.

Alima turned to her; "Please, Aunt Saadia please," she tried cajoling Saadia.

She took a while to mull it through. "Well, it would not hurt, I think."

"Okay, you can come along," Sarah finally agreed. "You have to assure me about one thing though, which is, that when you get to the market, you'll not wander around or get lost."

Alima quickly jumped into the van in excitement. Joshua and Sarah followed her, putting their seat belts on while Tariq drove off. Alima's excitement could be seen, having lived in the orphanage for a while, and it was the first time she was out. Alima embraced Sarah warmly for agreeing to take her along, before kissing her on her cheek.

"I want to thank you, Sarah," she humbly said.

"You're most welcome honey," Sarah replied.

Joshua couldn't help but smile. "Perhaps you can assist us in picking some good vegetables for tonight's meal," he asked of her.

Alima's face grew sulky instantly; "I don't like vegetables, but I'd prefer candy, and want one," she grunted.

Sarah interrupted, from where she sat; "Alima, candy is bad for you, and it ruins your teeth," she said in a motherly tone. "It's better if we get some fruit."

Alima seemed to fancy the idea of getting fruits as she bounced happily in her seat with joy.

"Yeah, fruit, I love fruit," she sang. "Can we get some dates?" "Of course, we can honey," said Sarah. "You can get anything good for you."

"You'll be able to find all the supplies you need when we get to the market," Tariq interjected. "It's a big place, and they have fresh fruits, vegetables, fish, and meat at very reasonable," he explained. "You can bargain with them also."

"I may get some dates then," Sarah said.

Alima sat up and peered through the window. She could see cars and trucks drive by.

"I love the farmer's markets. I was in one in Casper Wyoming where there were rows and rows of tables, and they sold organic fruits and vegetables, jellies and jams, pies and cakes, shirts, and made carvings and just about everything" Sarah thrilled them to help occupy time until they arrived at their destination.

"This may look like Casper but better," said Tariq.

They arrived at the market, and Tariq parked the car for them to get out. He unfolded a shopping cart with wheels and handed it over to Sarah. "You'll need this Sarah," he said

The market looked rowdy as they headed on. Most of the vendors were men while some wore comfortable clothing and others had either a kaffiyeh or head cover Most of the women walked up and down wearing a black hijab with a long black cloak which swayed back and forth as they moved. Their children followed them although the younger girls had no .hijab on, while the boys donned simple shirts and pants.

"Why do the young girls have the liberty of not wearing head cover and gowns?" Sarah asked.

"By Islamic law, it's not an obligation for a young girl to wear a hijab, but by the time she is of age "(baligh) Tariq explained to her.

"When she comes of age, she will be ready to wear the hijab." They had just gotten further, where there were lots of vendors with their tables and various items on them. They walked up to the first fruit vendor. The fruit vendor had all kinds of fruits, from bananas to melons, dates, persimmon, apples, oranges, grapefruit, and peaches. Sarah picked up some apples and bit into one. The vendor stared at her strangely as she took the bite from the apple.

"Would you care for a bite?" she offered Joshua.

Joshua looked at her worryingly; "You're aware you aren't meant to eat apples here without having paid for it?"

Sarah pushes the apple towards Joshua's mouth, trying to force him to eat it before Joshua grabbed both of her hands.

"This was initially the fruit of evil," he said.

"Yes, it was, but it makes a nice apple pie now," she chuckled. "Haven't you tasted Maggie's apple pie?" she asked in a tease. "No, I have not, hopefully soon," said Joshua.

Sarah asked the vendor to fill the bag she handed him with apples and paid him. She also asked him to pick some oranges, pears, and lemons just before Alima ran up to the fruit man and asked him for dates. Sarah smiled gently, pointing to the one she wanted.

"I like the giant ones," said Alima. "Do they have pits too?" "I have them with pits or without them," said the vendor. "We will then have five pounds of large pitted dates," Sarah said. Sarah paid the man, and he placed the dates inside the bag and gave it to her. Sarah placed the bag inside the cart. "Alima, let's go to another table."

"Do you like broccoli?" she asked the little girl. "It's perfect and advisable for someone your age."

Alima's disdain for vegetables was evident by her frown; especially broccoli which she disliked. She tried encouraging the little girl about the need to eat her vegetables, so she could grow strong and tall like she was. Alima couldn't risk not developing well for not eating her veggies, before grudgingly deciding to accept getting some.

By the side of the vegetable vendor, there was another vendor with wooden barrels of assortments of nuts, rice, and beans. Sarah looked down into all the barrels, and they were all filled to the brim with almonds, pine nuts, walnuts, sesame seeds, black beans, white beans, white rice, and red beans. "I will take five pounds each," she said. The vendor took his large metal scoop and dug into the barrels digging out the nuts, rice, and beans and placing them onto the scale. He began to frown, and sweat began to run down his face, nervously trying to figure out what would be the conversion between kilos and pounds. "Here you go said the man, I hope I got it right," giving Sarah a bag of each of the nuts, rice, and beans. Sarah gave him the money and placed the bags into her cart. Moving on, she came across a butcher with all kinds of meat and poultry. The poultry being mostly chickens were de-feathered and butchered, and some of them laid in whole stacked on the tables. Some of the chicken's carcasses hung on a string on top of the vendor's stand. Blood trickled down the body of the chicken and droplets of oozing liquid pooled on the vendor's wooden table. "It is our tradition to drain the blood out of the chicken." "It becomes halal, proper and legitimate," he said. "These poor chickens," Sarah replied.

"Would you like them cut in pieces or will you take it in whole?" he asked her. Sarah stared at Alima, and Alima stated at her back. "I think we will pass," she said.

Sarah journeyed around and came across a fish vendor who had different kinds of fish in a large metal bowl, with some already cleaned.

"Do these fish have scales?" Joshua took an interest in the cleaned fish.

"Yes, they all have scales," the fish vendor obliged him.

"Good, because I don't like eating fish without scales," he murmured.

Sarah chuckled before speaking to him; "I can cook the fish on the open fire for you to eat right away."

"That's kind of you, thanks but perhaps later. We are in a hurry," Joshua let his frown off with a smile.

Sarah pointed out to them about time and how little they had left to spend in the market. They visited a vendor dealing in hand-made carpets, bowls and numerous other articles to make some quick purchases, before heading off to another who sold children's wear.

She purchased some yards of cloth for them while getting some not too expensive but lovely dresses for the girls, and shirts for the boys. The children would be thrilled, knowing they will have new clothes, which was her intent.

She thought about clothes and about purchasing the best apparel for the kids. Then, they decided to call Saadia to know of their sizes. Saadia provided her with sufficient details, before asking that they get her a box of a dozen rose scented soap bars.

~

While Sarah was on the cell phone with Saadia, Joshua's eyes wandered away from the cloth vendor and across the market, where he saw a man covered in a hooded dark brown gown with a rope around his waist. His face was dark and heavily wrinkled, and the bone between his eyebrows protruded oddly. He lifted his arm and with his long index finger and long dark fingernails, pointed towards Joshua, indicating for him to come over and meet him.

Joshua walked towards the strange looking man to see what he wanted. He had gotten close enough to hear the man speak in a deep voice saying; "Jeshua long time no see. I know your Father sent you to this world on a mission."

He could recognize the man immediately.

"What do you want Satan? Didn't I tell you before to stop tempting me?" Joshua felt agitated as Satan began to snicker.

"Jeshua, calm down, all I came here for is to give you a second chance," he spoke treacherously. "I want you to join me in the world your Father has given me to rule over, where you can be of immense help gathering the people so they can worship me."

"Have I not told you, thou shalt worship only the Lord thy God, and serve him only?" Joshua indulged Satan with some biblical quotes he was aware Satan knew too well.

In a lower voice, he repeated; "Jeshua, Jeshua... People in this world will never follow you and your Father. They are corrupted and will continue to be that way."

Joshua chuckled at his lame attempt to sway him. "Satan, I will never follow you, and the days will come when people will not worship nor follow you," he taunted the furious looking Satan. "On that day, my Father will shackle you and toss you in the lake of fire as it is written."

"It will never happen," the furious looking Satan said. "You will eventually change your mind and bow down to me."

"I will never bow down to you Satan, or have you forgotten, that thou shall not test the Lord your God," Joshua reminded him in a high tone of voice.

Satan's breathing heightened as he said; "Well then let it be, and we shall see."

Joshua stared at Satan as his legs, arms, hands, and entire face turned into a shimmery of black and white smoke. He disappeared, and his brown gown fell to the ground. Sarah ran up to Joshua with an inquiring look across her face.

"Who was that and where did he go?" she asked curiously. Joshua smiled, turning to look at her with his face lightened as nothing wrong had happened;

"Someone was asking me for directions," he put. "I guess he was lost, but I could not help him."

"Do we need to get anything else"? said Joshua. "No, we got pretty much everything we need," said Sarah. "It is getting late, and we should be getting back," she said. They had all just journeyed back to the car, when they heard a high pitch humming sound, prompting them to look up to the sky where they could see a large silver color drone flying above them. The drone measured approximately 7ft long, and it had no markings on it.

It looked like a small airplane with long wings with a propeller on its back. Without warning, two small doors on the bottom of the drone opened, and a bunch of white flyers began to fall to the ground. Alima ran away from Joshua, Sarah, and Tariq with excitement to pick up one of the leaflets. Joshua picked up one that had fallen before them.

"What does it say?" Tariq and Sarah asked together.

Joshua read it out loud;

"We will find you in every house, behind every bush, and as Allah is our witness." "We will kill every one of you; because you infidels and Christians are nothing but Cancer to this Country."

oshua cringed. "That does not sound good," he said. Sarah was watching Alima pick up the flyers, and yelled at her, "Stop Alima leave those alone and come back here." There was a woman next to Alima, wearing a black gown and black hijab with her face covered and carrying a woven basket. She diligently began to pick up the flyers and stack them inside the basket until it overflowed. As she strolled towards the Vendor's tables, the flyers began to fall to the ground leaving a trail of flyers. Alima continued to pick them up. She lay down her basket on the table and turned around to walk away briskly and disappeared into the crowd.

Within a minute of her dropping the basket, a whining sound emanated from the basket. The whining pitch got higher. They heard a loud blast. Alima, just a few feet away from the explosion, was knocked down onto the ground. Some of the vendors' tables and tents caught on fire, and ambulances appeared throughout the market.

Sarah and Tariq froze in horror, unable to comprehend what had just happened. The shock was striking, and they could barely move. Sarah began to cry as Joshua ran up to Alima to pick her up. She was covered in blood but was still breathing.

He looked over to the ambulance which had just arrived, but they had too many people to attend to, that there was no time to help Alima.

"We need to get her to the hospital right away," Joshua said in a worried tone.

Sarah was jittery, and Tariq looked red with rage.

"Wrap her with some of the blankets Sarah purchased," Tariq advised him.

Joshua followed Tariq's advice. He rushed Alima to the back of the van where he laid her.

"Sarah, sit in the front with Tariq while I comfort her," Joshua ordered, picking her up in his hands and looking straight into her eyes while she took one more breath and then stopped.

She appeared dead, and he could feel her soul drifting away from her body. She finally let go, collapsing in his arms as she died. Alima's soul drifted away, appearing before an angel whom she looked at in a confused manner.

~

"Don't be afraid my little one, for I know you have lots of questions," she said in a calm tone. "I know of someone who has the answers to those questions, and I will bring him to you."

Immediately, she vanished with her, bringing her to a place she couldn't recognize, with so much light and in different colors. Across from her, there was a figure wearing a white gown. It appeared to be a man. He had his back turned against her. As she got closer, she began making out in better vision. The angel left her alone with the figure. She came up behind him, yanking the edge of his gown to gain his attention.

He turned around slowly, and it was Joshua whom she couldn't help but smile at saying; "Hello Joshua, what are we doing here and where is this bright place we're in?"

Joshua kneeled and took her hand.

"You're in another realm Alima, which only happens when people die," he explained to her, with tears dropping from her eyes down her cheeks as he spoke.

"Why did I die, Joshua?" she asked? "I'm still young and haven't even grown old yet," she struggled to understand the reason for her death.

"It's not your doing child, but one of evil itself," Joshua replied to her. "I will bring you back home, though, for it isn't yet your time."

～

Within the instant, she gasped back into life, coughing out loudly. Alima took one deep breath after another in the process to the sound of cars honking their horns and people talking. She looked at Joshua with solemn eyes. It became easy for her to believe she was alive and no longer afraid.

155

They finally arrived at the hospital emergency entrance. "I will go get a medic," Tariq said. He ran off and went inside and immediately came back with a medic and a stretcher to pick up Alima. Sarah looking down at Alima, grabbed her hand, and began to shed a tear. "Hang in their little one," she said, accompanying Alima. As they both walked into the main entrance of the hospital, Tariq looked at Joshua, worried sick, wondering if she was going to survive.

"Will she survive?" he finally asked Joshua, who lifted his arms into the air saying; "Only God can answer that question."

Joshua and Tariq saw many people in the lobby area waiting for a doctor. Blood rushed down their faces, arms, and body. Their bodies were severely bruised, and their skin charred. Most had bandages over their heads, legs, and chest. Most were bleeding and in excruciating pain.

"So many people are hurt, and I wish I could help them," he whispered, knowing he couldn't, or he would expose himself.

He could see the nurses running around; knowing bothering them was futile since they were short of staff. He walked up to the emergency room and found the door closed. Sarah was sitting down in a chair just outside the hospital room, patiently waiting to hear the doctor's prognosis. She laid her head down, and tears streamed down her cheeks. Her mascara and eyeliner slowly streaked down her cheeks.

"The doctor and nurse are looking at her right now, but I'm not sure she's going to make it," she sobbed hard. "She is still so young and innocent, and I haven't told Saadia because I'm meant to be responsible for her well being."

"Don't worry Sarah, you need to have faith in God, and he will heal her," Joshua tried convincing her.

"I am not sure if coming here was the right thing to do," she whispered.

Joshua sighed gently, easing into the seat next to her.

"God called us out here for some reason, and I know he has a plan for everything," he said.

Sarah lifted her head and wiped off her tears before smiling at Joshua. Joshua gently began stroking her hair while Sarah grabbed his hand and held it in a prolonged moment of silence before the doctor and nurse burst out of the room and walked up to them. "Hello, my name is doctor Sayed, and this is my nurse Arra."

"I must confess I'm speechless," said the doctor, while Sarah stared at him in confusion. "She is going to make it, and I still cannot believe it after the injuries she sustained," he said.

Sarah sighed relief. She looked at the doctor, who was utterly dumbfounded.

"She was badly cut up and bruised when she got here, but when we left and came back to take her to surgery, we did not see any sign of infliction or wounds," he narrated further.

The door to Alima's room opened suddenly, and the dimly lit room showed Alima on her bed with IV in her arm and the life monitor equipment attached to her. They walked in to see her with the doctor.

The doctor stared at Alima and said, "She must have had a guardian angel with her when the blast occurred."

The doctor shook his head and left. The nurse informed them that they could take her home as soon as she was awake. Sarah looked at Joshua, noting that he was right all along about God being with them.

CHAPTER 11

⚜

The Church Service in Bartella

It was the day of Church services, and everyone wore their best attire. Sarah exhibited a pleated fit flare red dress with medium-high beige color shoes. She looked into the mirror and began to style her hair in a bubble bun. She took a pencil and outlined the edges of her lips and then grabbed the ruby red color lipstick from her purse and began to put it on. She smacked her lips to make sure the color was even. Her blue eyes sparkled like blue diamonds and reflected onto the light blue eye shadow. Her cheeks were rosy red. She held a white Hijab in her hand, deciding whether to put it on now or later. "I guess I will wear this while driving to church and then take it off," she murmured. As she walked into the dining area, she met with Saadia. Joshua adorned, in his new suit, walked into the dining area as well at the same time.

The suit was painstakingly pressed as if it was just taken out of the dry cleaners. All of sudden Joshua came to a screeching stop. "Wow, Sarah, you look fabulous," he said. "I think all of the men are going to be staring at you today." "I feel the same way, said Sarah. I believe all of the women will be staring at you today as well." "You look like one of those models out of a fashion magazine," said Sarah. "Where did you get that suit?" "Oh, my father gave it to me." "He is a tailor, among other things." Sarah took her hand and ran her fingers under the lapel of the suit, "That is fine material," she said." It is made from the finest sheep wool," said Joshua. She paused, looking at him intensely and rubbed her lips. "Well, you look very handsome." "Thank you," said Joshua. Saadia slowly walked up to Joshua and held a small white rose with both of her hands. She stared at him as if she was love struck. She placed the rose on his lapel and winked at him.

"If I were your age, I would ask you to marry me." "I would consider your proposal," said Joshua. Joshua took Saadia's hand and kissed it. Saaida began to blush and began to tremble. "Oh, Joshua, you are so sweet." Alima wore the new dress Sarah bought for her at the market. The dress was pink and had a sweet lace and sequin bodice combined with a tiered, shimmery tutu-skirt. She smiled and ran up to Sarah and hugged her. "Don't I look pretty?" she said. "You're the most beautiful little girl I have ever seen," Sarah flattered her with a hug.

Saadia was feeding the other children their breakfast when Sarah asked Alima to join them at the breakfast table. Sarah had already told Saadia and the church group what happened at the market and of the miracle that came to be.

When Alima sat at the table, they all looked at her weirdly like she was a miracle child.

"Alima, you remember what happened yesterday?" Sarah decided to find out.

"All I heard was a big blast before I fainted and I don't remember anything other than Joshua holding me," she replied, staring at Sarah.

"Yes, he was the one who picked you up and comforted you while we took you to the hospital," Sarah noted.

Alima looked at Joshua, who was sitting next to her, thanking him with a smile. Saadia came in from the kitchen with a tray of an assortment of bread, fruits, cereal, glazed cream donuts, dates, orange juice, coffee, and tea. "We better eat soon, or we'll be late to church," she said. Brad stared at the food on the table then; he laughed out saying;

"The entire meal here is just enough for me. Do you have extras for the others?" while Ed, Carla, and Samantha began to laugh too.

Carla looked at Brad with a frown.

"Saadia you need to keep an eye on your kitchen or Brad will eat you out of house and home," she teased.

Samantha joined in, telling Saadia; "You'll need to take daily trips to the market just for Brad."

Saadia asked Sarah to help with the blessing before they began eating. Everyone bowed their head.

"Lord, thank you for saving Alima's life. Bless Saadia for making her food, as well as Joshua for helping us and bless the entire church group that came here to support us. We are humbly grateful in Jesus name we pray. Amen."

They all said Amen, and they began passing the trays of food around to each other. They began to talk among themselves while eating. Tariq came into the dining room wearing his best suit and looking radiant. "The vans are all fueled up, and I am ready to take you to Church, he said. "My, you look very handsome," said Sarah. "I think Joshua now has some competition," she stated while staring at Joshua with a smirky smile. Tariq began to blush immediately.

"We have several vans outside waiting for all of you, and Joshua, don't forget to get our bibles," he said to avert the discussion about his looks shyly.

Joshua headed off to Sarah's room, where the boxes of Bibles were on the floor. He picked one up and thumbed through the pages. He wondered how many times the phrases in its content had been changed, though similarly meaning the same thing. He put the bible back in the box and brought them all out one after the other. Brad, Ed, Carla, and Samantha all took the boxes of bibles outside and began to place them in the van. Alima grabbed Sarah and Joshua's hands and began to swing with excitement just before they got into the van.

~

They had just arrived at the Church to hear the bell ringing. It was a beautiful church made of stone and stucco. The doorways and the windows had arches. There was a pillar where the bell hung and across at the top front entrance. The vans drove close to the Church and Tariq, and the other drivers opened the doors to the vans. They all got out and began to walk toward the Church.

They approached two large wooden doors carved with a beautiful motif. On the door was a hefty brass door knocker in the shape of a hand holding a circle. Surrounding the circle was a motif. Upon entering the Church, they took a good look at the walls, which left them impressed with the architecture.

The church walls were made of stone and had many magnificent carved arches and pillars. The floors had a colorful mosaic of Christian symbols with crimson and blue colors and a picture depicting Jesus holding out his hands. The ceiling was vaulted, and the design features left them breathless. The people at the Church stood up upon their entry, turning their heads to look at Sarah, Joshua, and the other members of the church group as well as Saadia the children and Tariq.

They did as he asked before he began speaking again. "Today is a special day because we have guests from America," he smiled widely." They are our brothers and sisters from the state of Wyoming who has come here on a mission to bring their blessings and their help to the orphanage."

He introduced them to the Church, starting with Sarah the head of the group and the other members as they each stood up upon the mention of their names. Everyone clapped in appreciation. The Pastor asked for their eyes to be closed, as he led them into prayer;

"Lord, we thank you for bringing this missionary group here to help us and bless them for the work they will do. Lord, please, watch over them and ensure they get back home safe and sound. Amen."

Everyone said Amen as well.

"Today we will talk about Matthew in our books but before we do that let's all sing a hymn," he paused briefly, looking away from his Bible. "I'll also like to inform our guests of the tradition in our church, which means they will sing a cappella."

Everyone in the congregation chuckled aloud.

"The women will sing some verses while the men follow along," he explained. "We place the songs words and music symbols on the screen so you can use kindly all sing-along."

The congregation began singing. Sarah, Saadia, Alima, and the church group began to sing as well. Joshua stood to watch them. After two songs, the Pastor asked everyone to be seated. They obliged his request, settling into their seats nicely.

"Will you please turn to the chapter of the Gospel of Matthew in the Bible," he asked of them. "Who was Matthew? Did he ask? He was a tax collector, and his gospel is the most highly regarded gospel by the church fathers."

The entire Church began flipping their pages to arrive at the topic.

"He recorded most actions in the life of Jesus Christ, and it is clear and widely accepted that Matthew was written for the Jews." Evidence can be culled from Matthew Verse 5:17-18,"

he pointed out, asking someone to read from their book.

Don't assume that I came to destroy the Law or the Prophets. I did not come to destroy but to fulfill. For I assure you: Until heaven and earth pass away, not the smallest letter or one stroke of a letter will pass from the law until all things are accomplished."

Joshua, in a subdued tone, repeated the words as the Pastor spoke on.

"Therefore, whoever breaks any of these commands and teaches people to, will be called to justice in the kingdom of heaven," he warned them all. "But whoever practices and teaches these commands will be called great in the kingdom of heaven."

"What does this mean?" someone asked from the congregation?

"It means Christians should and must obey God's law," he replied. "An uncommitted Christian ceases to be a Christian at all and Jesus demanded obedience. I see and hear people every day saying since Jesus came into the picture, we are free to break the laws and do whatever we wish to do. This belief is a violation and an insult in Gods eyes."

Everyone in the congregation listened with intensity. The preaching stemmed around committing sins and not understanding how much damage it does to their souls. The Pastor emphasized further on different topics, before bringing the teaching to a close.

"Right now, we're going to have communion which is the sharing of bread and wine," the Pastor announced.

Ushers at the Church picked up trays and went around each row of pews to hand a tray to the person at the end. On the plate was a tiny glass of wine and in the middle of the tray, was a piece of flatbread the size of a small minute square. Each member of the congregation took a small glass of wine and held the bread in the palm of their hands. After all of the trays with the wine and the bread had been distributed, the Pastor said; "Let's all bow our heads and say the prayer of the bread."

"Heavenly Father, thank you for this bread of life we're about to eat. Whoever eats this bread will never be hungry."

Joshua, in a subdued tone of voice, began to recite the blessing of the bread in Hebrew.

> *Baruch atah adonai eloheinu malech haolam hamotzi lechem min ha-aretz"*

Translated it, he said,

> *Blessed, are You, Lord of our God, King of the Universe who brings forth bread from the earth."*

Everyone ate the bread and said Amen."Now we say the blessing of the wine," the Pastor said again.

> *Heavenly Father, we thank you for bringing forth this wine. Blessed art Thou, LORD our God, King of the universe, creator of the fruit of the vine."*

Joshua, again in a subdued tone of voice, began to recite the blessing of the wine in Hebrew.

> *Barukh ata Adonai Eloheinu melekh ha'olam borei p'ri hagafen."*

Translated, he said,

> *Blessed, are You, Lord; our God, King of the universe, who creates the fruit of the vine."*

Everyone drank the wine in unison.

The elders gathered the tiny plastic glasses of wine and laid them on the tray. The ushers brought in the tithe plates and distributed each one to the person at the end of the pew to pass down just afterward. Most people gave their tithes and those that could not afford to pay them passed on empty plates, after which the ushers collected the money and placed it all in a large jute bag.

Joshua eyed the person holding the jute bag. Overly worried, Joshua said to Sarah: "I sense a traitor in this congregation."

He looked towards the elder who was carrying the money bag but did not say anything.

"What do you mean by that? Why do you sense this?" she inquired. "Does he appear like a thief to you?"

She hadn't spoken long when the doors to the church were kicked in and opened wide.

A group of men wearing dark covers, dark shirts, and dark jeans burst inside with their weapons. They started to shout "Allahu Akbar," before one of them discharged an assault rifle into the ceiling. Bits of white stucco started to float down over the people's heads. They were being showered with snowflakes as it appeared. Those in the congregation began to shout in a frenzy, and the women and children began to cry loudly. Alima trembled, as she grabbed hold of Sarah, hugging her tightly.

"You are not welcomed in this house!" the Pastor yelled after the masked men had begun ordering the church members to head out of the church. The Pastor looked at them with rage in his eyes. "Let us be, you are defiling the house of God," he voiced as best as he could.

He had started making a nuisance of himself for the masked men, inciting the leader to remove his 357 Magnum gun from his belt. He points the gun at the Pastor's head, and the Pastor cringed with horror. "You don't make the orders around here," said the leader. He pulled the trigger of his gun ejecting one bullet, instantly killing the Pastor. The Pastor dropped to the floor, helplessly.

The shot prompted the whole church congregants to begin flooding out as they kept running as quickly as their legs could convey them. The elder who had collected the entire Church's tithe whom Joshua suspected for his activities earlier, ran off with the money.

The circumstance worsened, as more masked men rushed into the Church with sledgehammer and metal cans of gasoline as they desecrated the inside of the Church.

They began smashing the pulpit and the pictures before going on to destroy all of the pews. They broke the columns and began to pour gasoline all over everything before igniting the inside of the Church.

Some of the men gathered the bibles and took them outside the Church to place them in a pile. They formed the pile into the shape of a pyramid and poured gasoline over them. They lit the pile with a cigarette lighter and burned it. As the bibles burned, the leader fed the fire with more bibles. The smell of the burning books permeated the air. The blaze intensified, and he could feel the warmth of the fire against his body. He stared at the crackling fire and the white and black plumes of smoke as they rose up from the pile into the air. In celebration of his victory, he took his automatic rifle and held it high into the air. With exuberance he shot a series of rounds in the air shouting;

"There will no longer be any Church services here," he informed them with an evil laugh.

The other men took their sledgehammers and axes and began to break the cross symbols on the outer part of the Church. They took down the bell and left nothing but destruction in their wake.

The congregants were terrified and knew not what their destiny would be; on the off chance that they would be taken in as prisoners or their heads would be severed. They knew that being Christians, they had to pay the price for their beliefs. The men demanded that the congregants empty their pockets and they took possession of their wallets, watches, jewelry, and car keys. They made everyone remove their clothes and change into fluorescent orange suits. They were bound by heavy iron shackles on their feet and made to stand in a straight line.

The young girls were separated and told that they would be married off, especially those ranging from thirteen years in age upwards. The terrorist placed Joshua, Sarah, Tariq, Saadia, Alima, Brad, Ed, Carla, and Samantha into one group. The other Church congregants and children were ushered into another group and sent away. Joshua tried resisting before getting hit in the back of his head by one of the men. He had begun bleeding from his mouth as the man yanked him by his hair and roughly tossed him to the ground.

"If you dare defy me again, I will burn you alive," he threatened, calling one of the men to take Joshua away from the lot.

~

They lined them up and made them walk across the desert without any water. The COTT group began their journey. They did not know where they were they were being taken. As they walked, The weight of the chains and shackles pushed their feet into the soft sand, making it difficult to keep their balance. They were whipped as they dropped to their knees. They heard a snap and realized the leather strands of the whip ripped into the skin. The blistering sun began to hit their backs. The sweat trickled down their faces, and their lips became parched. They saw ahead of the convoy of their stolen vehicles while trekking the desert for several miles. A signal from the leader was given to halt. "Men, take the vehicles to the auction and get them sold, but keep the trucks," he said. They came to a halt, and the group stood there looking at each other and wondering what their final fate would be. They watched the leader walk across a few yards away and approach several giant dried tumbleweeds. The leader stood there silently, gazing at the weeds. "What is he doing said, Brad? Is he taking a leak"? The leader then exposed a large piece of tin roof laying on the ground surrounded by a dry grassy area and covered by sand and pebbles just a short distance from a large hill up north. The men approached it cautiously, helping him brush off the sand and pebbles with their hands and pull up the hidden doorway.

Upon getting it open, a dim light revealed a stairway leading down into a tunnel through which they forced everyone to go. Underneath, the terrorists led them into a passageway. The tunnel was cold and gloomy. At the end of the passageway, they came upon a makeshift prison cell the terrorists had built. The cell bars were made of rough solid iron and iron girders. Inside the cells, there were no windows to look out, and the only light they had, was a dimly lit light bulb hanging from the ceiling. The men began to corral everyone and pushed them one by one into the tightly spaced cell. "Hurry up, get inside; we don't have all day," said the man. The man closed the cell door and placed the key into the keyhole. He turned the key, and the clicking sound alerted everyone that the door was tightly shut. "This is your new home now because you are infidels, you will rot here," said the man. Sarah and the rest were terrified out of their minds as if they were ready to pass out any time. Brad yelled at the men while they were walking away. "You guys can rot in hell," he said. "Be quiet, they will take you away and execute you on the spot," Sarah said. "We will die in this cell anyway," said Brad.

The men weren't done with Joshua, grabbing him and placing iron shackles on his hands, before hitting him as hard on the side of his waist, as they could simultaneously, with the butt of their rifles in turns. They finally eased off, yanking him along to a separate cell, where they constructed a pulley of chains, which was tucked around his wrists.

He watched them with a badly hurt face and wounded pride, as they opened a large pit before him, previously concealed with two large wooden doors with a small hole in the middle. With the help of the pulley, they began lowering him into the pit, which he noted was dark, cold and damp.

"This will teach you not to disobey us," one of them giggled as he helped lower Joshua into the pit for his punishment. They took his walking cane and threw it inside the pit, and they closed the doors behind him. The men pulled the heavy iron bolt in the lock position and placed a large padlock.

Joshua remained still upon hitting rock bottom, making no sound, and casting no emotions across his face. The cell was quiet except the sound of a drip of water falling from the ceiling as well as the high pitch squeaking sound of a rat. He could recall his time when the Romans lowered him into a pit to spend the night before his crucifixion. He hung there, not knowing what his fate would be. Joshua heard the men chattered away, leaving him there through the night.

The following morning, they came to the pit hoping to get him back out. As they began pulling him out, they noted the chains felt light. They were wondering what was going on as they hastened their act to get to the end of the chain as quickly as possible. To their surprise, they found Joshua absent at the end of the chain. They picked up the shackles and angrily tossed them to the ground.

They took their flashlights and lit the pit but could find nothing. They were amazed at how Joshua could have escaped and where he could have gone. One of the men ran over to the leader to immediately make a report on the missing man. They quickly went to the jail cell area to see if he was around but found nothing.

The leader, frightening in appearance, and quite heinous to look at approached Sarah;

"Your friend is missing, and we cannot find him anywhere," he said to Sarah and the other church members. "It seems that we have a magician on our hands," he joked with a wicked laugh. "When we find him, his head will roll."

Sarah felt irritated by the disgusting cells. Their fate was unknown. They were hungry, and their bellies growled and rumbled. They hoped and prayed, only to receive information that soon they were going to be moved to another location by one of the men.

"Perhaps we all are going to be executed," Brad said. As Christians, they knew that they might have to die for their faith, but without knowledge of how and when it was to be. They heard cries and moaning sounds in the other cells next to them, but they could not see who they were nor was there anything Sarah could do to help them, and it broke her heart dearly.

CHAPTER 12

The Escape

That same evening, Sarah heard someone approaching the jail. She could make out a shadow and thought it was the leader of the terrorist group, ready to move them. She finally got a better glimpse of the incoming figure as he drew nearer. She then saw a silhouette, a man with a beard and long hair. Surprisingly it turned out to be Joshua.

"Joshua," she whispered in excitement. "I am glad to see you. How did you escape?"

"I picked the locks to the shackles and hid in the caves until sundown," he whispered back, looking around. "I came to get everyone out of here, but we have to be very quiet."

He took out a key from his pocket and placed it into the jail cell keyhole. He turned the key and unlocked the door. He signaled everyone with his finger to his lips to be very quiet. Alima ran out to Joshua, hugging his legs. She was trembling and began to cry.

He stroked her hair. "Be a strong dear, we will get out of here soon," he promised her.

He went to unlock the other cell but discovered that the people inside were dead.

They all quietly followed Joshua, walking through the dimly lit tunnel.

"Do you know where you are going," said Sarah. "I scouted the underground tunnel and found the exit before I came to rescue you," he said. As they moved forward, a dribble of sand fell on their foreheads. The sand ran down their faces, over their mouths, and onto their chins. They wiped the sand with the sleeve of their shirts. "The ceiling above the tunnel is not very stable," Joshua said. Sarah felt something slither by her. She heard a hissing sound. "Could it be a snake, or am I just imagining things," she said. "It could be a cobra," said Brad. They are all over these deserts. "Be quiet, Brad, you are scaring Sarah," said Samantha. "I am beyond scared," said Sarah. As they continued their journey, the tunnel began to narrow, and the ceiling became lower. , and they had to bend their heads to avoid hitting them. Joshua came up to some narrow wooden stairs. "I believe we have reached the end of the tunnel," he said. Joshua walked up to the stairs and put his hands on a thick tin plate. "This must be a door," he said. He pushed the tin plate upward with great force. Upon opening the door, a cool breeze hit his face. It was dark outside, and the little light they got was from the emanating glow of a harvest moon and the stars flickering high up above.

One by one, they all walked out of the tunnel. "Is everyone ok," said Joshua. They all nodded in silence with a sigh of relief.

"We need to move on," said Joshua. They walked across the desert with no GPS or maps to follow. The only light they had to guide them was the moonlight. It was a chilly night sending cold shivers down their spines. Their hands and legs became numb, and their legs stiffened. From a distance, they could hear the cry of the Arabian wolves calling from the horizon. As they walked, the sound became louder, and they feared they were going to be attacked by them. Sarah and Joshua lead the group, and Saadia was behind them holding Alima in her hands since she got tired and could not walk anymore.

"I never expected this would happen to us," Sarah confessed in a weary tone to Joshua.

"Sometimes it happens for a reason," Joshua beckoned her to have faith. "The father is always testing us to see if we have faith in him."

"What is going to become our fate?" Sarah asked. "Are we getting out of here alive?"

"Sarah, I can't answer your questions," Joshua sighed "The father in heaven has a plan, and he chooses his people, just like he chose the Jews."

He did his best to let her know God sticks with those who remain faithful to him and never doubt his actions.

"We have to move on until we can find the next town," said Joshua. They walked all night until they saw the sun rising over the horizon and just a little distance away, they saw a town.

"Let's stop there, we might be able to find food and water there," Joshua thought.

They finally arrived in the town, and they could not see a soul. All of the buildings were dilapidated. The roofs to the buildings were either missing or collapsed. The buildings inside were severely burned, and the windows were either split or missing. There were bullet holes riddled throughout the exterior walls. In the middle of the square, there was a pile of burned wood and ashes and the smell of creosote in the air.

Sarah looked down and saw a couple of burned skeletons as well, screaming and grabbing Joshua before looking away. "Oh my God, what on earth happened here," she said. The corpse appeared to be of two men burned alive. Brad looked around the empty square, unsure if they were alone.

"Is anybody here!" he yelled to gain some attention, with his words echoing twice with no answer.

Joshua asked Brad, Ed, Carla, and Samantha to scout for food and water. He asked Tariq and Saadia to stay with Alima while they all scouted the area. The scouting party walked ahead, through a corridor and upon the end found a building without doors. There was a metal plaque on the building and what they would gather by reading it appeared to be a school. Remnants of ashes and burned wood laid on the floor.

They found a lantern on the wall and preceded their walk to the second level by the stairs that creaked as they climbed them. Once they reached the second floor, they manage to light up the hallways. On opposite sides of the hall, there were doors with frosted windows. Some of them were busted, and as they peeked through, they could gather that the rooms were classrooms due to the many student chairs, a teacher's desk and chalkboards.

"Let's see if they have a kitchen," Brad gushed, heading forward.

"He is always looking for food," said Samantha. "He must have two stomachs, unlike the rest of us."

Samantha located a solid core door without a frosted window on it, which she thought to be the kitchen. She let it opened slowly, unable to see anything within the room, she struggled to walk through. The room smelled terrible and felt quite cluttered, as she kept bumping into something. "What a peculiar odor, it smells smokey," she said. "There must be some furnishing or boxes in my path," she mumbled. Just as she kept walking something pointed pricked her, leading into a scream.

"Brad, Ed, Carla, come here quickly," she yelled as they came to her aid with their lantern.

"What is wrong?" said Brad. "Something touched me. I can't see what it is," said Samantha. Brad took the lantern and held it up high. Hanging from the ceiling on a hook, was a skeleton inside a cage. The skeleton was scorched, and its hand had been protruding from the cage. Brad moved the lantern in the other direction and saw a scary sight. More burned skeletons in similar cages hanging from the ceiling around the room. They counted no less than twenty skeletons.

"This is sick," Brad said. "Let's get out of here," Ed said, sounding terrified.

"No, we have to find some food and water," Brad objected, asking them to move on. "Let's stay together."

They walked up to another door and slowly opened it. Inside, they saw a large kitchen with pots and pans hanging from the ceiling as well as a large stainless steel refrigerator.

"Ed, you open up the refrigerator?" Brad asked.

"Why pick on me?" the scared Ed queried. "There may be something dead inside."

"Hopefully something dead we can eat," Brad whispered. "Yuk!" said Carla. "You will eat anything, won't you?"

Brad gave Ed a nudge to go ahead, but he refused to be pushed. He slowly opened the door with one eye shut. The stench of rotting moldy food greeted them warmly as he did, making them step backward.

"This really smells bad," said Ed. "I feel like throwing up," he noted, quickly shutting the refrigerator door.

～

Joshua walked into a building a bit dingy and with light coming in from the fallen roof. He saw a bunch of empty wooden cages before looking up to the roof to see a large opening. The rafters were hanging down, and the sun was shining through. He stared at the sun and squinted. He could tell Brad, Ed, Carla, and Samantha was not going to find any food or water.

He opened the doors of the cage and began to pray. In a matter of a few minutes, a flock of quails started to come down through the roof and flew into the cages. He looked around and found two urns of water, and he placed his finger inside one of them and turned the water into sweet wine. He took his finger out and put it into his mouth.

"This is tasty," he said. "I think this wine will be the best I ever made."

Joshua yelled for Sarah to come to see what he had found. She obliged his call, running over immediately from the other room. The quails made a crowing sound as she stepped in the room.

"That's odd," she noted. "How did they get there?"

"Maybe someone raised them for food. Look, I also found two urns," Joshua showed Sarah.

"Is that wine?" she asked astonished.

"You can taste it to know for yourself," he encouraged her. "Let's gather some wood for the fire and ask Saadia and Tariq if

they can help us prepare the meal," she advised, helping him carry the items over.

He grabbed a sack and opened the cages to pick up the quails and place them in the bag. They went back to the courtyard where the scout crew had just come back gloomy and with sad faces. They had gotten nothing.

"I found some quails, wine and water," Joshua said to them, watching their eyes widen in the process. They were left amazed by his finding after theirs was fruitless.

"Joshua, you're a life saver," Brad sighed. "God truly blesses you."

Evening dawned upon them, as they set up a campfire. They had found some iron rods and placed the quail on the rods and began to roast them.

"We don't have any plates, cups, forks or knives," Sarah worried.

"I saw some at the school building kitchen earlier. I'll go and get them," Brad offered.

"I will go with you," said Ed. Brad and Ed went back to the school building to pick up the plates, cups, and utensils. "Are you afraid of going back the schoolhouse?", said Ed to Brad. "Not really," said Brad." We did not find anything except a bunch of dead people". "Aren't you afraid there may be a ghost?" Sarah admitted she saw one, said Ed. "I never saw one; therefore, I can't believe in them," said Brad. "I haven't seen one either, but when I do, I will most likely shit in my pants," said Ed. When Ed and Brad returned, they saw the quails roasting on the rods. The glowing fire began to crackle and sparkle as the quails cooked. The smell of the sweet aroma of cooked quail made their mouths salivate. "Boy, that smells good. I am famished," said Brad.

There were enough food, water, and wine for everyone to consume that evening. After the meal, the group sat around the fire and expressed thoughts about their mission.

"This place gives me the creeps," Sarah shivered, thinking about the environment, while aching for something sweet and comforting to eat after her meal, like chocolate and melted marshmallows.

"Same here," Carla confessed. "We found a room at the school with burned skeletons inside cages hanging from the ceilings." "She narrated, watching them feel uncomfortable. We didn't want to tell you about it before our meal."

"Oh my God, those barbarians," Saadia cried in hurt.

The sky was full of stars, and it was a chilly night. Sarah was looking up when she noticed a shooting star pass by.

"Did you make a wish?" Joshua asked.

"Yes, I did, and I wished we'd all get home alive," she divulged.

"Don't worry Sarah, provided we aren't in the hands of the terrorist," Joshua assured her.

Ed returned with a large metal bowl in his hands. He had found the large bowl in the kitchen and made indentations around it with a hammer. "What do you have there?" Sarah said. It's a hang drum. "Have you ever seen one or heard one?" Ed said. He took the metal bowl he had found and placed it upside down on the ground and began to beat it with a rather large iron mallet. He put the bowl on his lap. He began to tap the impressions he made on the side of the bowl and began beating on it, making a pleasing sound that everyone enjoyed.

They temporarily forgot about their worries, while he played until the fire died out and they fell asleep.

CHAPTER 13

⸎

The *Rescue*
That morning, Joshua and Sarah lay sleeping on the ground, both embracing each other, besides the smothered fire. They felt someone kicking them hard.

"Wake up," the voice said.

They struggled with the sun shining brightly on them, making it hard to distinguish who the person was. They became startled but noticed that the person wasn't wearing black. There were more than one eventually, wearing green camouflage uniforms and berets each with a patch on it and the shoulders. They all carried rifles with scopes as well, while some carried machine guns.

"Who are you?" Sarah asked, courageously.

"We're from the special forces of the Iraqi government," said the Commander in charge, who made his face well seen by bending over to them.

They were even more startled, helping themselves to their feet.

"What are you guys doing here?" the Commander asked? "We

just escaped from terrorists," Sarah explained." They attacked and desecrated the town, including the church." "Where was that exactly?" the Commander wanted to know. "Bartella," Sarah replied.

"Bartella?" asked the Commander out loud. "It seems they've advanced more than we felt they would," he murmured.

"They killed most of the people in the town, and we're the only ones left," Joshua explained. "They took us as hostages and made us walk for miles."

"They took us down into a tunnel," Sarah joined in on the explanation before the Commander cut in.

"Do you know where the tunnel is?" he asked sternly.

By the looks on their faces, it was evident Joshua and Sarah had no idea how to get to the tunnel. They informed the Commander that they had moved through the night and couldn't locate it in any way.

"That's how they've been able to bypass us and get ahead faster," the Commander kicked against a stone in his path.

Sarah could tell he was angered by the thought and wanted to catch terrorist by any means possible.

"I think we might be able to trail our footsteps back," she stared at Joshua saying. "Although, I don't want to go back and I just want out of here."

"If you can take us halfway to the tunnel, I will call a convoy and have them pick you up and take you to the airport," he assured them.

"You got yourself a deal," Joshua extended his hand to meet with the Commanders. "When do we leave?"

"Our men are tired, so we will rest here today and venture out tomorrow," he replied

The guards took their canvas tents from their truck and began to pitch them on the ground. They took wooden poles and ropes and laid them down to prop up the tents once they had placed the stakes down. Joshua was watching one of the soldiers curiously as he took a hammer and began to pound the stakes into the ground.

He relived the painful experience of when he had his hands nailed to the stake with a hard driven nail. With each strike from the guard with his hammer, he could feel his hand nailed to the cross, in a loud cry. With the second hit, he could feel his other hand nailed hard into the stake painfully. Sweating profusely, Sarah interrupted Joshua by tapping him on his shoulder.

"Are you okay?" she asked.

"I'm fine, I was Just watching the guards put up the tent," he responded with a deep breath.

"They told me our tent is ready, but they are going to separate us," she explained to him. "They set up several large tents in which one is for the women and the other for the men."

He nodded his head, thinking it was reasonable.

"Alima, Samantha, Carla Saadia, and I will be sleeping in one tent. I guess you guys are all sleeping together," she sighed. "Just a word of caution, I was told Brad snores, so you better get some cotton for your ears."

"I get claustrophobic at times." "I think I'm going to sleep outside," Joshua informed her with a blank face.

She felt something was odd about him.

"Are you sure?" she asked in an overly concerned manner. "It's going to be cold."

He brushed it off with a smile.

"I enjoy sleeping outside and watching the stars while I doze off," he gently nudged away her concern.

The soldiers began passing out duffle bags with blankets and pillows. Joshua got one too, before walking away a few yards from

Sarah's tent and kneeling on a mound of sand. He lay down the blanket and duffle bag before lying down. While he had his back to the ground, he counted the stars and knew the names of all of them.

In the depth of the night, a beam of flashing light began to emanate above Joshua. His father's voice came roaring through in warning of the day ahead;

> Jeshua, you will be faced with the enemy tomorrow, and they will want to destroy you. Show no emotion and anger and kindle your frustrations. Be strong and stand up to them for the ones that will want to destroy you are Satan's armies. I will always be by your side, for I know what the outcome will be. I created time for I am the alpha and the omega. Honoring me is the greatest gift any father could have from his son as you have always done. I miss you and hope to see you back in the kingdom soon".

That night, Joshua, with no worries whatsoever, slept like a baby, waiting for the big day ahead.

CHAPTER 14

Back to the Tunnel
The next morning, the armed forces packed their gear and began to head out. The rest rode in the open face truck, while Joshua and Sarah rode in the back of a 4x4 jeep with the Armed forces commander and his driver. They had driven forward a few miles when a sand dune caught Joshua's attention.

"That dune looks familiar," Joshua said.

Upon getting closer to the dune, they heard a whistling sound from a rocket, launched next to their Jeep. More missiles followed, with a second almost hitting their truck.

"Everyone quickly gets out of the trucks!" the Commander commanded.

The troops began to form into a circle prompting Tariq, Joshua, and Sarah to take a position at the back of the truck while helping Alima and the others from the truck one at a time. The Commander waved to Joshua to come over immediately. Joshua hurriedly ran up to the Commander.

"We don't know where the rockets are coming from, can you pinpoint the possible location of the tunnel from here?' he asked, running short on the breath as he gasped

"I'm not certain, but I think we're getting close," Joshua said, looking up at the sky.

The rockets being fired finally stopped.

"We need to scout the area to locate the entrance." "I am going to need you to go with me, Joshua." "I promise to bring you back."

Sarah offered to go along, but Joshua stopped her, noting it was too dangerous and she needed to remain with Alima and the group. "Joshua, please don't go," she said, bowing her head and looking down at him with a soulful look. Joshua took her hands and embraced them with his, trying his best to comfort her.

"Everything will be fine," he promised with a smile. "It's best if you stay here to offer your support to the group."

Sarah looked back at Alima, who looked so terrified and in need of comfort. "I think you are right; I will stay."

Very loudly, she yelled; "But you better come back Joshua Elo, or I will personally come over to find you and drag you back alive or dead," as he walked away.

The Commander requested for the radio, calling the command center for some more reinforcement. "We need twenty gallant troops to escort us," said the Commander.

Joshua and the Commander waited for the convoy of troops to arrive. Within minutes they assembled in one line. "Troops follow me and keep your eyes open. Joshua, you follow me," said the Commander. Joshua and the Commander hopped into the Jeep. They drove many miles across the parched desert. The blazing sun beat down on them without mercy. The desert haze and the slight blowing of the sand made it difficult for them to see. Their sweat began to pour down their heads, onto their eyebrows and eyelids and distorted their vision. They both squinted their eyes and noticed an image over the horizon. Without further ado, they saw a black flag pop up behind a dune and heard the revving sounds of motors from numerous small pickup trucks. As they rushed toward Joshua, the Commander and troops, the tires on the trucks began to spin on the dunes and throw piles of sand behind them.

As Joshua and the Commander fixated their eyes on the trucks, they noticed that the trucks were equipped with bazookas and automatic Gatling guns. The trucks began to advance closer to them. There were just too many of them. They were outnumbered by far. Joshua looked at the Commander and noticed a frown on his face. He radioed for the soldiers to stop and retreat. Respecting his request, they started to drive back.

However, they had paid little notice to the trucks coming from both sides. They had seen them too late. While bearing black flags, the terrorists did well to have their faces covered as they approached wearing black uniforms. They opened fire immediately, shooting bullets above their adversaries' heads, while the Commander cowered in fear.

"We have you surrounded, and you can either surrender or have your brains splattered," the terrorist leader ordered for their surrender.

The military vehicles finally stopped moving and getting out of their trucks; they were all promptly disarmed by the terrorists. The Commander's troops dropped their rifles and put their hands up in the air. The terrorists immediately ran up to the soldiers and picked up the released arms. The leader of the terrorist group walked up to the Commander of the Iraqi army, staring down at him.

You're a disgrace protecting these people, and for that, you'll never defeat our army," he boasted. "We are greater than you, and we will take away your lands, women and children and all of the infidels."

He walked away, turning his back and raising a finger to the sky; "Kill them all including their leader!" he yelled.

The terrorists began lining up the troops side by side, including Joshua and the Commander. Joshua stepped in front of the group, and he shouted at the top of his voice; "What do you have to do with me, don't torment me."

The terrorists cocked their rifles, stepping back before they began to fire. All of the troops, including the Commander, fell to the ground, except Joshua who remained standing. They concentrated their guns on him like they had missed earlier, shooting with rage, but he continued standing and undaunted.

Their leader returned in rage, grabbed his gun, and ran up to Joshua firing at him but to no avail as the bullets bounced off of him. The terrorists began to look worried; wondering how he was able to defy the weapons. Sternly Joshua raised his cane and wove it from left to right, turning their leader's gun to nothing but dust that trickled out of his fingers down to the bloody sand.

He turned towards the other terrorists, doing the same, and dealing them the same fate. They held the dust in their hands and looked down upon it as it slid through their fingers. They looked terrified as they approached their leader with their hands held high.

"You fools! It's nothing but magic," he screamed at them. "Get back there and apprehend him."

Joshua waved his cane once more, dealing them a different fate this time by turning them all into dust and letting them fall onto the ground from the air where they hung temporarily, except for the leader who was struck with fright.

Joshua walked up to him with no fear in his eyes and no worry in his heart. In a loud and thunderous voice, he said. "My father made you out of the dust, and in the dust, you will return to the earth upon which you stand," he grinned.

He defeated the leader with a wave of his cane into dust like he had done his troops. He took a good look at the Commander's soldiers who had fallen upon the ground after being hit with bullets. Deciding not to bring them back to life, and keeping to his Father's instruction not to bring someone back to life if they saw them died. He commanded the earth to cover their bodies by mixing it with sand until they couldn't be seen anymore. He began to make his journey back to meet Sarah and the rest of the group. That day he crossed the desert with no food or water. He smiled upon remembering the time he fasted and wandered in the desert for 40 days.

It was hot that day, and the scorching sun was beating on him, and he had begun to sweat while the wind whipped against his face violently. This time he was not led by the Holy Spirit but had come to be there because he was caught in the middle of a war against religion, greed, and hate. He could have asked his Father for comfort in a meal, some bread and a canteen of water, but Sarah and the Church group would question him on how he got all of those necessities while in the desert.

Darkness fell upon him, and there was no place to seek warmth, nor did he have any means to build a fire. He was tired as he lay down against a large boulder upon which he rested his head while gazing at the stars. Beneath the howling wind, he could hear a wolf cry from the distance. He listened to the wolf getting closer to him. In a matter of minutes, a huge wolf appeared to him and started to snarl at him. The wolf showed its razor sharp teeth and seemed to be ready to attack Joshua. The wolf was not a normal Arabian wolf but rather to some degree, bigger. "That is weird, Arabian wolves do not hunt alone but in pairs or groups of about three or four animals," Joshua said to himself.

He remained perturbed, as the wolf began to morph into another figure. He was tall, with brownish red skin and had two large wings, goat-like horns sticking out of his forehead with a protrusion between his forehead, and wearing a nicely trimmed goatee. He had a long tail with equally large hands, large feet, and long nails. The figure before him was Satan. He flapped his wings and began to pace the ground in opposite directions. In a low tone, he began to speak to Joshua.

"Give up your hope for the people of this world for they will never change," he spoke in self-assured certainty. "They will always be corrupt, and you should let your father destroy the world."

"No," said Joshua loudly. "There will always be a few in this world that will not be tempted. They will resist corruption and lead themselves to the path of righteousness."

"It is too late," Satan said. "You cannot persuade people to change. Give up your hope and dreams and join me. Tell your Father there is no proof of salvation. You and I can reign over this corrupted world until he destroys it, and you can help me to build another world where people can enjoy doing their wicked deeds."

"Satan!" he called out loud. "The world I build and reign over would be a world of peace, tranquility without any sins, and upon this rock, I will build my church and the faithful will come and seek me."

Satan looked furious, unlike ever before. He walked at a furious pace to and fro before looking back at Joshua and pointing at him.

"Upon that rock, you will die. You have failed many times, and you will fail again," he chimed in anger. "Your father could have saved you back then, but he chose you to die."

"It was in his plan for me to die, to stop the corruption and forgive people for their sins," Joshua shot back immediately.

"Jeshua I will ask you again, come and join me," Satan tried his luck once more.

"Don't tempt me!" yelled Joshua at the top of his voice.

With a trembling voice, Satan said; "You will come to reason soon enough," disappearing afterward.

CHAPTER 15

W*ar against Joshua*
The following morning was a clear day, and there was not a cloud in the sky. The sun's rays shimmered onto the desert's soft pillowy dunes. Joshua began his walk back to Sarah and the group. As he walked on the desert, his shoes picked up scoops of sand with each step. Every step became harder and harder, and he used his walking cane to support himself. His walking cane sank into the soft desert sand on every level. He kept moving, walking toward the highest ground on the next rise of the sand dunes. All of a sudden, he heard a rumble in the sky.

As he gazed up at the sky, he could see several jets pass by over his head. The aircraft left a plume of smoke in their wake before returning to begin to move toward him once again. Upon their approach, they began to launch their rockets, which did nothing but hit the ground on both sides of Joshua without even hurting him. He looked up at them again and saw another group of jets fire upon the other aircraft that had just tried to kill him.

He couldn't tell who the good ones were, from the bad, but he had a plan set at heart to find out.

While the jets passed by Joshua, he took his walking cane and pointed it towards them and swung it in a side to side motion. The jets immediately turn into sand, leaving the pilots in midair, in sitting positions. As they plummeted from the sky, they open their parachutes. Joshua once more transformed their parachutes into the sand. As they tumbled to the ground, Joshua immediately took his walking cane and swung it again, making the desert hills turn into globs of shimmering green gelatin.

The pilots who cried out for the Lord to save them, landed softly on the globs and their lives were spared. Those that did not ask for the Lord's help, nor had any faith, landed on the ground, meeting their deaths immediately. The spared pilots walked away happy and could hardly perceive how the globs of gelatin showed up.

Joshua heard the sounds of engines in the distance. He turned around and got a glimpse of at least 100 or more trucks coming his way. Automatic machine guns were mounted on the trucks as well as anti-aircraft guns. Behind the trucks were men dressed in black with their faces covered. They all held riffles and walked on foot. Some of them held a black flag.

It was apparent as they got closer, they appeared to be terrorists. They looked angry and began yelling as they neared him.

"Allahu Akbar," they screamed atop their voices, rushing towards Joshua like a charging rhinoceros.

Joshua stood still with no fear and held his ground. He cast his eyes on the horizon. With both hands, he lifted his walking cane high up into the air. Clouds began to form, and they billowed across the sky, casting the desert into a shadow of darkness. Ripples of lightning bolts split the sky, and booming thunder could be heard. A gust of cold wind began to blow heavily, causing a dust bowl. The desert sand hit Joshua in the face, arms, and hands, scraping his skin as if someone aimed a sand-blasting gun at him. The ground began to tremble, and it felt like an immense tremor had hit the region. The terrorists lost their balance and began to fall to their knees. The desert ground cracked in a zig-zag formation and ripped open. In a boisterous voice, Joshua yelled at the terrorists, "YOU WILL NEVER CONQUER US." The sand on both sides of the crack, began to rise high, uplifting the terrorists and carrying them and their trucks, like an ocean wave pulling them up and pushing them toward a shore. As the sand took their footing, the dunes began to pour them inside the crack. Joshua heard the moaning and cries of the terrorists as they plunged to their death into the bottomless pit. When no more terrorists could be seen, the crack began to close slowly, and it sounded as if a concrete burial vault top was closing on them. Upon the clearing of the air, no terrorists could be seen, prompting Joshua to put down his walking cane slowly.

~

He continued on his journey to find Sarah and the group. As he strolled far in the blistering sun, he felt the sweat beading on his forehead. His lips became parched, and his tongue began to roll. His eyes narrowed into slits. From a distance, he saw a blurred image. The sun was distorting his vision and made it difficult to figure out who it was.

He finally made out a jeep coming toward him. The Jeep encircled him and stopped before a man came out and introduced himself.

"Are you Joshua?" he asked.

"Yes, I am. How do you know me?" Joshua asked back.

"I've been looking all over for you." "Sarah and the group asked me to help find you, and pointed me in the direction you took, which I followed here," he explained. "My name is Lieutenant Mustafa."

Joshua shook his hand briefly.

"Where are the Commander and his men?" he looked around Joshua asking?

"They all died," Joshua muttered painfully and with a concerned look.

"How did this happen?" Mustafa sought a better understanding. Joshua narrated the ordeal as best he could before the Lieu-tenant attested to him being saved by God. Mustafa headed back to his Jeep, taking out a canteen and giving it to Joshua, which Joshua opened without much ado. He poured the cold water over his head and face before drinking a little out of it. The coldness of the water slid down his throat as he quenched his thirst. "That is a relief," said Joshua. "Thank you very much."

"Come with me, I'll take you back to the rest of your friends," he beckoned Joshua, who climbed into the Jeep, and they drove off.

They drove for many miles on the desert and passed through rough, uneven limestone plateaus cut by wind and depressions strewn with loose flint like rocks. From a distance, Joshua got a glimpse of an array of arched metal buildings. As they got closer, he could make out many hangers and airplanes. He also saw many tanks and open jeeps with machine guns on them. As they drove by, a group of about 30 men, lined up in three rows, were running with their leader running in front of them. A little further down, the men were practicing some drill runs. They built an obstacles course of open wooden boxes with barbed wire on top. Joshua overheard the sergeant yell, "Men lay on your stomach and crawl through." "You have one minute to cross; otherwise, you will have to do it over again."

"This is our base," said Lieutenant Mustafa. "We took over this area last year, but the terrorists have been advancing south, and we may just have to move soon again."

Sarah spotted Joshua from a distance first, thanking her stars, and grinning happily to see him. She ran up to him, yelling his name from afar without a care in the world.

"Sarah!" he yelled in response, embracing her into his arms in a hug.

"I'm so happy to see you," she said, staring into his eyes. She pressed her lips softly against his parched lips. Looking around his body, she saw he did not have wounds. "I thought you were killed. We waited for you, and they told us it would be best for us to go to the base," she let out her breaths hard. "I'm just glad they found you."

"The terrorists killed the Commander, but I luckily escaped," he eased her nerves.

"I don't wish to be here anymore," Sarah sighed with bitterness in her voice.

"Where are the others? Are they all okay?" Joshua asked. "They're all good, but Alima has missed you so much," she informed him. "Alima has been badly terrified and hasn't spoken for days." "Maybe she'll start talking when she sees me," Joshua shrugged.

"Come with me," the Lieutenant said. "You must be hungry. Let me get you to the Mess Hall." Joshua followed the Lieutenant into a large metal arched building.

Inside there were many long tables.

"This is where our army eats," he said to Joshua. "I will have the cook prepare you a special meal."

With a wave of his hand, Joshua declined; "It is not necessary he said." "Don't be so modest. You were in the desert for a very long time without food or water," the Lieutenant tried persuading Joshua. "Please eat and get some rest."

The Lieutenant called the Chef and out he ran from the kitchen to the eating area.

"Prepare Mr. Joshua and his friend a meal," he instructed, to which the cook indicated his compliance with a response, before heading back into the kitchen.

Sarah joined him shortly, and they sat down at the table.

"It is a pity people in this country have to live with so much fear," Sarah sulked. "I heard numerous stories from some of the men here about how they lost their loved ones and had to abandon their homes and career to fight against the terrorists."

"I'm sure God will punish them for their wicked ways," Joshua spoke.

The doors of the kitchen opened and out came the Chef with a mezza, an assortment of appetizers and salads on a large tray. The tray was decorated with hummus, tabbouleh salad, and pita bread, that he just finished making. He also added some stuffed grape leaves, falafel, kalamata olives, and some dates.

Joshua stared at the tray. "This looks just like a meal for a King," he acknowledged.

"We treat our guests like Kings," said the Chef.

Joshua grabbed a piece of pita and broke it into the half before silently praying and then dipping the pita into the hummus. He felt the taste explode in his mouth, before offering Sarah some." This is good, try some," said Joshua.

"No, I just finished eating a few hours ago," she declined to say. "I will have a date though," she added, grabbing a large madool date.

Joshua grabbed the other half of the pita bread. He then took some olives, falafels, stuffed grape leaves and stuffed them inside the pita bread. He then took a spoon and slopped some hummus on them until the hummus began to drip on both sides of the Pita bread. He then topped it off with some tabbouleh. He proudly lifted the large sandwich he made to get everyone's approval. "This is my infamous king sandwich," he said. "You can make them back home and sell a lot of them," the Chef said. "That's a good idea; you can get your self a food truck and start selling them," said Sarah. Joshua and Sarah stared at each other and began to laugh.

That evening, Joshua and Sarah were in the middle of the compound, looking for the Captain to ask him when their plane would be ready to take them back home. Sarah saw the Captain near the plane, hangers speaking with his corporal. "Wait here, Joshua," Sarah said. Let me talk with the Captain. She ran up to him quickly and waved at him.

"May I speak with you?" she asked of him.

"You certainly may," he beckoned.

"I want to know when we can leave," she asked.

"We have a plane ready and fueled, but we can't leave until we get the authorization from our central unit," he explained while staring at her. "We were told the enemy are flying their planes nearby and shooting down ours."

She could understand his concern, thanking him for his time and patience, before turning around to leave with a worried look smeared across her face.

Sarah immediately reported back to Joshua. "I got some bad news, the captain told me we could not leave, until they get clearance from their central unit." "It appears that the enemy planes are flying in the area and he is afraid they will shoot us down." "That does not sound good, Joshua grumbled. "I hoped we could leave soon. I don't feel safe here," said Sarah. I feel the same way," Joshua said. "Let's inform others." Like two reporters reporting news on a flash event, Joshua and Sarah walked up to the guest quarters where Brad, Ed, Carla, Samantha, Alima, Tariq, and Saadia were staying. As they walked through the doors, Alima saw Joshua. Her eyes opened wide, and she ran up to Joshua, screaming with joy, "Joshua, you made it back. I missed you so much". "I missed you too," said Joshua. She grabbed his waist, laid her head on it, and wrapped her arms around him like an orangutan holding her infant. Sarah gazed at Alima. "This is the first time she spoke since she got here. She is so happy to see you". Alima grabbed Joshua's hands and started to pull him towards the table. "Come here look what we are playing." Tariq and Saadia sat at the table playing a board game. The board game was sumptuously decorated with shells carved with lapis lazuli and limestone, and the squares were all covered with geometrical designs. Brad, Ed, Carla, Samantha, and Alima surrounded them, watching them with intensity as if they were watching a world championship chess competition.

"What are you guys doing"? "Are you casting lots"? said Joshua. "No," Tariq said. "This is an intense game that requires the utmost concentration. It is called the Royal Tombs of Ur; it is similar to your game of Backgammon. "That sounds interesting," said Joshua. "This game dates back as far as the twenty-sixth century." I can't believe they have one here," said Tariq. The objective in this two-player game is to move every one of the pieces onto the board, at that point move them around the board, lastly off the board before the adversary does as such.

On the chance that the player arrives on a space possessed by a solitary adversary's piece, they send it back to the beginning. If the player comes on a space occupied by at least two of the adversary's pieces, then their piece backpedals to the beginning. "That sounds complicated to me," said Sarah. "No, it's not, come and try it out," said Tariq. "If I play that game, you might as well bury me in a tomb," giggled Sarah. "I feel he already buried me," said Saadia. "He won many times, and I am no match for him." "Perhaps Joshua can beat him." "Well, Joshua, what do you think?" said Sarah. "I can give it a try." Joshua sat down and began to play with Tariq. He knew he could beat him, but gave him the benefit of the doubt. As Tariq was making his move, the Captain burst into the guest quarters and disrupted their game. "You are clear to leave the base first thing in the morning, report at 10:00 hours he said". "Wonderful." said, Sarah. "Praise the Lord," Brad said. "Amen to that," said everyone.

CHAPTER 16

S arah's fate
That early morning, Sarah's attention was caught by a person riding a motorbike and wearing a white cap, and robe like the one she saw in her dream in Bartella. On the back of his bike, he had a hot box where he kept his bread. He stopped his motorcycle next to the metal building compound where most of the soldiers were congregating. He was yelling; "Fresh pita bread and hummus...free samples. "I'm going to buy some, so we will have something to eat on our trip back home," Sarah told Joshua, approaching the man.

"I just made the pita bread this morning, as well as the hummus," the man said to her, opening the box and showing her the bread and the hummus.

Sarah picked it up, and it was warm and tender to the touch. "Go ahead, try it," said the man. "I like it very much," said Sarah? "How much"? "1,000 Dinars per dozen," said the man. Sarah took some money out her pocket she had that had been given to her by the Captain to pay for some necessities at the Military store.

"I will have a dozen," she said briefly. "I'd like some hummus too," she added, trying not to forget. "Please try the hummus," the man said. "It is a Kalamata olive hummus." Sarah took a bit of hummus and dipped the pita bread into it. She put the creamy sensation into her mouth and savored it. "This is good," she said. "1,000 dinars for the container of hummus," he said. "I will take some," she said.

"I also have goats, cheese, and dates. Would you care for some?" the seller enticed her with a good business sense.

"Yes, please," she said politely. The man took a large sharp knife and pointed it to her face. She looked at him frantically and began to tremble. A cold shiver ran down her spine. "Is he going to slit my throat with that knife?" she said silently. The man then pulled the knife away from her and cut a sliver of feta cheese and placed it on the end of the blade. He then puts a seedless date on it. "Go ahead, try it," he said. Sarah slowly took the cheese and date of the knife being careful not to cut herself. She places the sliver into her mouth. "I like the saltiness with the sweetness together," said Sarah. "Good. I am glad you like it. It is a great combination," said the man. The cheese is 3,000 dinars and the dates 2,000 dinars. "I will have a half kilo each," she said.

"Yes, of course," added the man.

Sarah gave him some dinars, and he placed the bread, hummus, cheese, and dates in a white paper bag. She began walking back to meet Joshua, while the other soldiers ran over to the man's calls to patronize him just as Sarah had.

They surrounded him and began to shout; "Yes, we want to get a free sample."

"Of course you may have some free samples, I will offer you

what you deserve," he giggled while passing out the samples. The man pulled out some cheese and hummus. "Would you care for some cheese and hummus too"? Said the soldiers. They began to spread the cheese and hummus on their bread and began to savor the samples. "This is the best pita bread, cheese, and hummus I tasted said one of the soldiers." "I am glad you liked it said the man." "Take as much as you want." Take it all," said the man." The man kept distracting the soldiers allowing them to take everything he had.

He watched them pay him no attention, before pulling out a cord from underneath his gown. He tugged on it, resulting in a massive explosion. The sound heard was like a heavy cannon fired across a field. Blood splattered over the metal building. Bodies, including the merchant, were dismembered, charred, unrecognizable and tossed in every direction, from where the merchant had stood with his motorcycle. From a distance, Joshua had a somber look on his face as he saw a pillar of dark smoke floating toward the sky. He could hear many jeeps revving their engines and the warbling sounds of ambulances as they rushed to the scene. A speaker high up on a wooden pole began to squeal, and then everyone began to hear an announcement. "Condition red. Terrorist on alert". The soldiers started to run in all directions chaotically.

～

As Sarah slowing walked towards Joshua, a sharp serrated object emanating from the blast flew behind her and struck her in the back, knocking her forward onto the ground. Joshua and the group immediately ran up to her and surrounded her as she lay on the ground breathless. One of the ambulance drivers spotted Sarah and drove up to her. A young man with dark curly hair, dressed in a white jacket with red medical emblem patches sewn onto it and sporting a well-trimmed mustache, rushed out of the ambulance. "I am Doctor Abdullah he said," pushing his way through the group. "Excuse me, please stand aside," he said.

He bent down and placed his fingers on her neck and applied slight pressure hoping he could feel a pulse. He then took out his stethoscope and put it on her chest. He patiently listens to her heart, hoping that he would hear a single beat. He turned her body over and saw a pool of blood on the ground and the red stain on the back of her clothing. He took a few seconds before wearing a horrible look. He shook his head and said, "She is dead," he whispered.

There was an intermittent silence, and then they all wailed profusely, as they let out streams of tears which rolled down their cheeks. They couldn't believe they had lost their dear friend in such a cruel manner. The group continued to cry but could do nothing but pray to God and ask for compassion and forgiveness for her sins.

CHAPTER 17

The Journey back home

They placed Sarah's body in a black body bag on the tarmac, alongside the supplies to be carried in the plane's cargo bay. Before boarding her onto the plane, Joshua requested that he see her one more time. "Please wait. I want to pay my last respect to her," he said with a heavy heart. The ramp agents picked up the supplies and placed them inside the cargo bay of the plane, leaving the body bag to pick up last.

Joshua walked up to the body bag looked down upon it, bending to unzip it just enough to expose her head slowly. She looked very pale as he planted a kiss on her head and remained in deep stare at her. Very slowly, and miraculously, Sarah opened her eyes slowly and then took a deep breath. She remained still for the next few seconds, staring right back at Joshua as a tear trickled down her pale cheek.

She weakly spoke in a shallow tone;

"What happened to me, Joshua? What am I doing inside this bag?" she asked.

"I need you to listen to me, Sarah," he called her attention. "Everyone here saw you die, and I cannot allow you to live again after that, for I intend for you to live in the kingdom with my Father and me in eternity when I return."

Sarah acknowledges Joshua decision. Slowly took her final breath before closing her eyes. Joshua closed the body bag and signaled for those arranging the loads into the cargo bay to take her away. He looked distraught but tried not to be, for she had a better place to be. Joshua slowly zipped up the bag. The military men picked up the bag and loaded Sarah on the conveyor belt. Joshua stood on the tarmac, watching the bag being loaded into the plane. He displays a solemn face, and he bowed his head down and began to pray. He wished he can bring Sarah back to life right away; however, he would have to wait for the right time. Brad, Ed, Carla, Samantha, Tariq, Saadia, and Alima walked up to Joshua, and they each embraced and hugged him. They gathered into a circle and held each other hands. They all began to pray. Tears flowed down their faces. We better start heading back home, Joshua said. Tariq, Saadia and Alima, I will ask the Government to allow you to come back with us.

CHAPTER 18

The Funeral

Upon returning to Wyoming, the Church and congregants had begun the preparations for Sarah's funeral. The Church had donated the money for her burial and decided to have a natural burial on a high ridge overlooking the mountains for her. They chose a burial plot for her in a beautiful pasture next to a large, old tree.

The Pastor's assistant constructed a large tent and placed it on top of Sarah's plot. They rolled a red floral carpet on the ground and put rows of metal folding chairs. They took the Church's podium and placed it in front of the chairs. Maggie donated a bouquet of pink roses and a large floral wreath on a wire, metal stand, to the sad event. The floral wreath was interwoven with red and white carnations and lemon leaves. On the top was the abbreviation inlaid in gold "R.I.P."

In the evening, everyone in the Church gathered around Sarah's casket with never-ending tears flowing from the church members who all loved her for her beautiful heart and personality.

Alima wept to no end, from where she sat on Maggie's lap. Samantha, Ed, Brad, Carla, and Joshua stood up, refusing to sit down while the Pastor went up to the podium to speak.

"Dearly beloved we are here today to say farewell to Sarah who gave her life to the church and for her vision to help children whose parent's had died as a result of being victims of war and repression," he sadly said, fighting to hold back the already pouring tears. "We praise her in death for her courage and determination to help those in need. We all will miss Sarah, and we know she will be in heaven with the Father and his son."

The entire church members fell silent as Joshua walked up to the podium. He had a few words to say;

"I just wish to say how proud I am of those who went on this mission to Iraq with me," he began. "As a Christian, we always suffer as it is necessary to pass through many troubles on our way to the kingdom of God."

Sighs aired around with people struggling to contain their pain and anguish.

"God put you here to do good even if it means suffering just as Christ suffered for you. He is your example, and you must follow in his steps," he shared with moving words.

Joshua walked up to Brad, Ed, Carla, Samantha to tear off a piece of their clothing individually. Brad looked confused, whispering to Ed to ask for Joshua's reasons for tearing part of their clothes.

"I think he is upset that Sarah died," Ed shrugged.

Gently, they began lowering the casket into the ground as Joshua started to say the mourner's kaddish, a prayer in Aramaic and Hebrew.

> Yitgadal v'yitkadash sh'mei raba b'alma di-v'ra chirutei, v'yamlich malchutei b'chayeichon uvyomeichon uvchayei d'chol beit yisrael, ba'agalauvizman kariv, v'im'ru: 'amen."
>
> Y'hei sh'mei raba m'varach l'alam ul'almei almaya. Yitbarach v'yishtabach, v'yitpa'ar v'yitromam v'yitnaseh, v'yithadar v'yit'aleh v'yit'halal sh'mei d'kud'sha, b'rich hu, l'eila min-kol-birchata v'shirata, tushb'chata v'nechemata da'amiran b'alma, v'im'ru: "amen.
>
> "Y'hei shlama raba min-sh'maya v'chayim aleinu V'al-kol-yisrael, v'im'ru: "amen."
>
> Oseh shalom bimromav, hu ya'aseh shalom aleinu V'al kol-yisrael, v'imru: "amen."

Translated, he said,

> *Glorified and sanctified be God's great name all through the world which God has made by God's will". "May God establish his kingdom in your lifetime and amid your days, also, inside the life of the whole House of Israel, expediently and soon; also, say, Amen". "May God's incredible name be honored perpetually and to all eternity".*
>
> *"Blessed and praised, glorified and elevated, extolled and respected, venerated and commended by the name of the Holy One, blessed be God,*

beyond all of the blessings and hymns, praises and reassurances that are ever spoken in this world; and say, Amen".

"May there be wide spread peace from heaven, and life, for us furthermore, for all Israel; and say, Amen".

"God who makes peace in God's divine statures, may God make peace for us and for all Israel; also, say, Amen".

While Joshua continued with his prayer, everyone took turns with the shovel and began throwing a piece of dirt into the hole. As the dirt fell down the hole, it dropped on the wooden casket in the burial vault, making a clunking sound. Alima threw a pink rose into the hole with her eyes barely able to open with so many tears gushing through them.

The casket was finally lowered entirely into the ground, and the cemetery workers were left to complete the filling of the hole.

CHAPTER 19

J oshua returns to the Kingdom
Joshua turned his back and began to walk toward the top of the mountain ridge. Brad was the first to take note of him.

"Where is he going?" Carla asked first while Brad stared. "He loved Sarah," Samantha sighed. "I'm guessing he needs some lone time and is very upset," she suggested as they watched his back become more and more distant from them.

Joshua arrived at the top of the ridge and stopped. He looked at the horizon and could see the sun starting to set. The rays of the sun hit his eyes tenderly, and he squinted. He looked down upon the ravine noting the drop was no less than a thousand feet. Below a river flowed rapidly.

Silently, he began to communicate with this Father. "Father he said, I have concluded my investigation." "There is hope for this world." "There are a few righteous people left, that are not leading a path to corruption and yet trying every conceivable way to conquer evil." "Those people will be worthy of your kingdom."

"They are powerless against the evil one, and we will have to return to help them." "Good must conquer Evil." He had just almost concluded his message when Alima ran up to him and stopped briefly.

"Joshua! Are you all right?" she yelled, asking from a distance. Joshua paid her no attention as he dropped his cane to the ground and raised both of his arms to his sides. He lifted himself, took a deep breath and like a man jumping off a ledge with a bungee cord, he jumped off the ridge and plummeted into the deep ravine. Upon his drop, he majestically began his ascension back into heavens in a shimmering glow of white light.

Alima looking terrified quickly ran up to the edge of the ridge after Joshua, but Brad was quick enough to apprehend her. He had followed her up the mountain and had gotten there just in the nick of time. She struggled as best as she could to gain freedom from him; kicking wildly and crying out loud.

The scene attracted a crowd, who all came to the edge of the ridge immediately to know what had happened. They searched thoroughly for Joshua, but they could not see him. Brad picked up his cane with a heavy heart, taking one good look into the distance.

"The poor fellow took his own life to reunite sooner in heaven with Sarah," he sighed. "I'll inform the authorities to begin the search for his body," he informed them all as they whispered and murmured about the occurrence.

With their heads down and chanting prayers, they all walked back to the church saddened about the death of their two dear friends.

THE END

EPILOGUE

From a view of outer space, the planet earth is slowly rotating. A few distances away, a giant asteroid twice the size of the Earth is gradually heading its way to destroy Earth. As it gets closer, the massive asteroid is diverted, and God tells Joshua in a deep, solemn voice. I built seven new worlds for the believers. Those that believe in us and adhere to our Laws and Statues will inherit my new worlds. The world will be a sanctuary. There will be enough room for them to live in eternity. As promised, I will also resurrect those that believe in us, including their families, friends, pets, and beasts in the world that did no sin or repented for their sins. I will let them all dwell with their beloved and allow them to live in peace with no burdens, no labor, no illness, and I will provide them with food and water. I will leave behind on Earth Satan worshipers and those that are corrupt to defend themselves.

www.ingramcontent.com/pod-product-compliance
Lightning Source LLC
Chambersburg PA
CBHW031316040426
42443CB00005B/95